D1077622

More Frantic Semantics

Further Adventures in Modern English

John Morrish is a freelance writer who worked on *Private Eye* and was editor of *Time Out*. He also trains new recruits to journalism, where an interest in the meaning of words sometimes proves helpful.

ALSO BY JOHN MORRISH

Frantic Semantics
Snapshots of our Changing Language

John Morrish

More Frantic Semantics

Further Adventures in Modern English

PAN BOOKS

First published 2001 by Macmillan

This edition published 2002 by Pan Books
an imprint of Pan Macmillan Ltd
Pan Macmillan, 20 New Wharf Road, London N1 9RR
Basingstoke and Oxford
Associated companies throughout the world
www.panmacmillan.com

ISBN 0 330 48452 4

1 3 5 7 9 8 6 4 2

A CIP catalogue record for this book is available from
the British Library.

Typeset by SetSystems Ltd, Saffron Walden, Essex
Printed and bound in Great Britain by
Mackays of Chatham plc, Chatham, Kent

Foreword

When I was at school I used to spend part of the summer holidays working for the family television firm, accompanying the engineers as they went to people's homes and performed major surgery on the stricken box in the corner.

Some of these men had trained on wireless sets, but it was a matter of professional pride not to let the new technology – printed circuits, valves, painted wood cabinets – trouble them. On those rare occasions they decided to consult the manual, they would do so with great ceremony. 'Let me look in The Book of Words,' they would say, before plunging their hand once again into the warm bowels of the sick receiver.

I have always loved the phrase, which apparently appeared spontaneously in the 1930s, when these men were children. It is gently ironical about the printed word, but reveals an ingrained respect: something to do with chapel, lantern-slide lectures and self-improvement, probably. Of course, just about every book is a book of words, unless you count books of matches and 'graphic novels'.

But this is a 'book of words' in the most literal sense. It's full of them, and it's about them: new words, altered words and old words doing new jobs. Every picture may tell a story, but every word *is* a story. In these pages you will encounter tramps, circuses, tadpoles, space exploration, handwriting, jazz, wife-swapping, confectionery, mysticism, cheese, madness and herring. Among other things.

Both this volume of *Frantic Semantics* and its predecessor deal with our changing language, a proposition no one could dispute. Readers of the *Telegraph Magazine*, where versions of these pieces first appeared, certainly do not. Many write to me about these changes, usually to protest.

In discussions of this type, it is customary to introduce a distinguished list of commentators who have had similar complaints, from Kingsley Amis, W.H. Auden and George Orwell back to Swift, Johnson, Defoe and Dryden. All wondered whether the English tongue was becoming slack, if not actually slobbering. Then, having brought them in, it is equally customary to declare them wrong, if

I

not ridiculous. Look, runs the argument, we are still speaking English, aren't we?

That does not make them wrong. When Dryden complained about imported French phrases, or when Defoe bemoaned swearing, or when Orwell denounced 'prefabricated' phrases, they were all doing jobs that needed doing *in their own time*.

It is sad for us if our contemporaries can't understand Shakespeare – although people in other English-speaking countries seem to manage – but it is perhaps more important that they understand their prime minister, their bank manager or the writing on a packet of pills. Most of those who criticized linguistic change in the past were not doing so on behalf of the past: they were doing it so that people in their time could speak clearly and be confident of being understood.

Criticizing developments in English is perfectly legitimate, even if some of the perennial complaints are nonsense. Hopefully, people will soon realize that there are no reasonable grounds for objecting to the use of 'hopefully' to mean 'I hope'. It is perfectly acceptable to sometimes split an infinitive. Sentences may start with 'and'. And using slang, in context, is cool.

On the other hand, when politicians and bureaucrats say 'I refute that', when they mean they simply deny it, and interviewers fail to challenge them, because they don't know there's a difference, a valuable word has been lost. Worse, it has become a dangerously slippery word. To refute is really to disprove by argument, to the satisfaction of someone other than yourself. People who misuse the word are misleading the public, either deliberately or through stupidity. People will always lie, but it is better for everybody if they know they are doing it. But when words float free of meanings, that cannot be assured.

On the other hand, if English started to improve, how would we know? Newspapers would receive letters praising DJs for their informed use of the subjunctive. Everyone would speak like the cast of *Genevieve*. But in reality, many people's idea of an improving language would be one that gave them ever more subtle, ingenious and undetectable ways to deceive. On that level, English is thriving.

Actually, it's thriving on most levels. The English lexicon grows unstoppably, not least because of the ease with which new words are invented and used. It is a language that tolerates considerable grammatical unorthodoxy and improvisation. And that, probably, says something about those who speak it.

Thus the language of Shakespeare, Swift, Johnson, Darwin, Orwell and, er, David Beckham continues onward and upward. If it is not the most spoken language in the world, it is the most spoken language in the wealthy half. But through the Internet – technophobes may like to take a nap at this point – it may push that triumph until other languages are crushed. Already, half of the world's 5,000 or so languages are on their way to the boneyard, mainly because the children who should be speaking them are joining Mr Sting in his reedy chorus of 'I want my MTV.'

Like it or not, our changing language is changing other peoples' languages. If, indeed, it is *our* language. Our connection with English is historical, not proprietorial. The English language is like Cheddar cheese, and we know how much that has to do with Cheddar. We might like to think of our Cheddar as the original, but New Zealand, Canada and Ireland make it too. The version of the English language the world buys is American.

American English is all over this book. It is hard to say why it has suddenly become so dominant in Britain. When most of us were at school, we used 'American' slang at our peril, but loved it all the more. Did not America invent the great passions of the twentieth century: cinema, jazz, rock 'n' roll, organized crime?

But those Americanisms were fun. The new ones are compulsory. The new technologies are US-based, as are the businesses they have spawned. Those who invent things get to name them. We named the beam engine, the steam engine and the differential engine (whatever that was). But since the extinguishing of the white heat of technological revolution British ingenuity has concentrated on tweaking our secret weapon: irony.

I like America, and American culture, though I can live without access to a powerful handgun. But in the eyes of US corporations, British English is less important than Finnish, Persian or Korean. If I type 'colour' into the Help box of my beloved Apple Mac, it ignores me until I change it to 'color'. This is worse than inept, it's a creeping linguistic disenfranchisement. Still, the linguistic traffic is not all in one direction. We did give them 'shag'.

Those who deal with America or the Internet – much the same thing – learn to read and write both versions. The spoken word, though, is harder. Hollywood films are increasingly difficult to decipher, and we can't always blame quiet dialogue and loud explosions. Personally, I get the drift but I don't get all the words. It's perhaps just as well I'm not required to be interested in hip hop.

Educated, sophisticated Germans, Spaniards and Italians have lived with this for years. They understand English and yet they don't. In the future, some say, everyone will speak English and their own language. English will be what Latin was to medieval Europe: the official medium of business and government. Everyone will have two languages: except us, as usual.

And what will global status do to our language? Already, children from Kent and Cornwall to East Anglia and Gloucestershire are speaking with the same accent, a kind of 'Cockney Lite', tricked out with words and syntax from Jamaican patois, Australian backpackers and Mancunian DJs. The speakers understand one another, but those outside that sociological niche may only be able to decipher the swear words.

As someone whose grandparents spoke a Bristolian so pungent that it required subtitles – except for other Bristolians, usually – I lament the loss of regional English. But I don't want to speak like that. There are only so many times a sophisticated urban professional can stand being asked about the whereabouts of his tractor.

While putting together *Frantic Semantics 2*, I read two fascinating books. Simon Winchester's *The Surgeon of Crowthorne* is, in part, a biography of James Murray, the man who created the *Oxford English Dictionary* with the help of nothing more complicated than hundreds of volunteers, countless little slips of paper and a tin shed in the back garden. The second, Steven Pinker's *The Language Instinct*, shows how modern science threatens – or promises – to do away with that whole humanistic tradition, in which language was studied by acquiring lots of books and concentrating very hard indeed.

What makes it worse is that Pinker, basing his magisterial overview on experiments using countless kindergarten children and powerful brain scanners, makes a strong case – and does so with admirable lucidity and wit.

Pinker's thesis is that language is innate: almost everything we need to start speaking and listening is etched into the circuitry of our brains. We just have to start up the system by making contact with other language users at a key stage in our development. Once we do so, the wobbly pink blob between our ears lights up and soon we are a regular on *The Moral Maze*.

Language is innate, because we evolved that way. And all human languages are fundamentally similar despite their surface differences, because they, too, are a product of evolution through natural selection. Some people are apparently trying to reconstruct the single language they claim *Homo sapiens* once spoke. Apparently, the disinterred vocabulary runs to forty-one words: more than enough for some dinner parties.

All of which means, Pinker seems to suggest, that the appropriate approach to changing language is just to observe it, like watching weather, birds or trains. We may prefer people to write 'use' rather than 'leverage', or 'We will benefit in two ways' rather than 'It's a definite win-win scenario for us', but those are matters of taste and etiquette. He compares them with table manners.

On this, though, I'm with George Orwell, whose scientific expertise didn't run much beyond keeping chickens. In his famous essay *Politics and the English Language*, he attacked 'the half-conscious belief that language is a natural growth and not an instrument which we shape for our own purposes'.

Language may evolve, but every human soul – not a scientific term – chooses how to wrap its thoughts in words. All variants of English may be of equal scientific validity: but outside the laboratory, as Orwell knew, some languages are more equal than others. You may have your natural language, the language of your family, your tribe, your caste. But you may not want it to define you or, as Orwell says, to 'think your thoughts for you'.

Steven Pinker doesn't like 'wordwatching' either. 'For me,' he says, 'wordwatching for its own sake has all the intellectual excitement of stamp collecting, with the added twist that an undetermined number of your stamps are counterfeit.' This is harsh, not least on stamp collectors, some of whom have gone on to lead quite useful lives in the community.

Personally, I like watching words, and thinking about what they tell us about our times. Of course, the remarks that follow have only made their way on to the page by a process of natural selection. I hope you enjoy them, while sparing a thought for those not fit enough to survive.

Once again, I would like to thank the *Telegraph Magazine*, where these articles first appeared. In particular, a word of praise for Denis Pigott and Lucy Hyslop, whose tussles with language in the subediting department rarely receive the praise they deserve. I would also like to thank the many *Telegraph* readers who have written to me with comments and ideas. I do appreciate every one, even if I don't always have time to reply.

Thanks also to Catherine Whitaker, my editor at Macmillan, for long-distance support and American neologisms. I'd also like to thank Suzi Feay, at the *Independent on Sunday*, for letting me review the odd dictionary, even though I increasingly find their plots rarely match up to the cast of characters.

Michael Quinion (www.worldwidewords.org) and Jonathon Green continue, in their different ways, to show me how it should be done. Green's alarmingly huge *Cassell Dictionary of Slang* is my new best friend, after the *OED*, of course. And thanks again to the press office at the Oxford University Press for keeping me up to date with their other reference books.

I would also like to mention two publications, one on old-fashioned paper and one on the Internet. The quarterly *Verbatim* (www.verbatimmag.com) is a tremendous non-technical read for anyone interested in language. Meanwhile, the Internet *Vocabula Review* (www.vocabula.com) takes language mavenism to extremes, and contains some of the ugliest 'elegant writing' yet encountered. Frighteningly reactionary, but oddly compelling.

Finally, I'd like to express my appreciation to friends and family, especially Tony Bacon – no, I don't know why we say 'bog standard' – and Harrison Sherwood, struggling so hard against the terrible handicap of being American. And finally love to my wife, Deborah, and my two boys, Edward and Freddie, who have been kind enough to provide me with a living primer in language acquisition and social constructivism. Now stop answering back, the pair of you, and clear up that mess.

@

One of the leading characters in modern life doesn't even have a name, unless you count 'commercial at'.

But anonymity has not prevented @'s rise to fame. Since establishing itself as the common element in every e-mail address, it has become a fashionable component of tee-shirt slogans and book titles: consider Bill Gates's *Business @ the Speed of Thought*. (It's all right: you don't have to read it.)

The ubiquitous squiggle has plenty of nicknames. The computer folk who rescued @ from its lonely vigil on the top line of .the typewriter sometimes call it 'the strudel', although others prefer 'the vortex' or 'the whorl'.

Elsewhere in the world, there are exotic variants. Here are a few from an article by Karen Chung of the LINGUIST Internet mailing list (http://linguistlist.org/issues/7/7–968.html): 'the monkey's tail', 'the elephant's-trunk-A', 'the miaow sign', 'the maggot', 'the little dog', 'the cinnamon bun', the 'rollmop' and 'the snail'.

Thais, meanwhile, call it 'the wiggling worm-like character', which must make passing on your e-mail address a long job.

The symbol was apparently invented by medieval scribes as long ago as the eighth century. To save space and quill strokes, they abbreviated the Latin *ad* – meaning 'to' or 'at' – by looping the tail of the 'a' around the letter.

As a commercial symbol, it was first used by sixteenth-century Italian merchants. But in English it came to mean the 'at' in such expressions as 'five barrels at a shilling each', found from the seventeenth century, and later took its place on the typewriter keyboard.

In the twentieth century, columnated invoices and accounts threatened its future. But it was still considered essential for the first computer keyboards, despite its effective redundancy.

In 1971, the e-mail pioneer Ray Tomlinson needed a symbol to separate the names of computer users from their addresses. He found it, dormant on his keyboard, and awarded himself the first modern e-mail address: tomlinson@bbn-tenexa. But he wasn't alone for long.

Access

Have you noticed the rise of the verb 'to access'? 'Students may access the library at the following times', 'To access the building press the button'. Or, much worse, 'I will have to access my head of department about that.'

Here 'to access' is short for 'to gain access to'. There is no logical reason to object to nouns becoming verbs. It happens all the time in English, especially with new activities: 'I'm going to email it to you' is one obvious example, but it previously applied to 'I'll telephone you' and before that, 'I'll telegraph you.'

But we don't need a new word for visiting a library or having a word with the boss, especially one so ugly. It is designed to give the speaker an air of technological competence. The verb 'to access' appeared first in 1962, when A.M. Angel coined it in his unput-downable *Large-Capacity Memory Techniques for Computer Systems*. To 'access' something in this sense is to retrieve information from a computer's storage area so you can work on it.

Soon, however, the experimental verb had escaped from the lab. In 1986, the *Daily Telegraph* made it respectable, mentioning an American company trying to 'access' new markets in Europe.

Meanwhile, the noun 'access' (fourteenth century, from the Latin *accessus*, meaning 'an approach' or 'a visit') has acquired new nuances. There are 'access' courses to help people with no qualifications enter those universities which still require them. And in politics, to have 'access' to ministers is to have influence over them. As if . . .

'Access' is also the term used by the divorced dads you see in the park at weekends, desperately trying to bond with their children during their allotted hours. 'What's your access like?' they ask one another. Symbolically, whereas 'access' was once pronounced like 'success', now it sounds like 'heartless'.

Angel

Barely a week passes without some small business looking round for an 'angel' to help it out. A rather earthbound role, but these days 'angels' must earn their keep.

A 'business angel' is rather like a 'theatrical angel', someone willing to lose money by investing in plays. Perhaps such 'angels' hope to hobnob with the cast in their brief moment of glory between finishing rehearsals and looking for a new job?

Business 'angels', on the other hand, are experts rather than philanthropists. Their willingness to use the title is a reflection of New Age enthusiasm for 'angels' of all sorts, from au pairs and office cleaners to celestial beings with the power to fight incurable diseases and find lost car keys.

In the Old Testament scriptures, the Hebrew word for 'angel' is *mal'ak-yehowah*, meaning 'messenger of God'. The Greek version, created *c.* 150 BC, used their own word for messenger, *angelos*. That was then borrowed by Latin and the Teutonic languages.

Originally it had a hard 'g', which explains St Gregory's famous joke. On seeing some blond Anglo-Saxon boys in a Roman slave market, he quipped, *'Non Angli, sed Angeli'*: 'not Angles but angels'. Well, you had to be there . . .

Initially, English stayed close to the scriptural meaning: a heavenly being, working for God. By the sixteenth century, however, it was possible to speak of 'angels' in a rhetorical sense, meaning 'good fortune'.

Later, kind people could be 'angels'. The Victorians liked this idea: the key text is Coventry Patmore's four-volume epic of marital bliss, *The Angel in the House*.

Business and theatrical 'angels', however, are American. The word turned up in a slang dictionary of 1891, defined as: 'one who possesses the means and inclination to "stand treat"'. Commercial and theatrical versions soon followed.

But when your 'business angel' comes calling, try not to ask for a bag of boiled sweets.

Antsy

'When you are interviewing people, do you find they get antsy?' A difficult question, especially if you're not exactly sure what 'antsy' means.

Context helps. The speaker, a young Englishwoman, obviously meant 'wary' or 'suspicious'. But what kind of word is 'antsy'? An adaptation of, say, 'anti'? Or something to do with 'anxiety' or 'angst'?

Luckily, 'antsy' is in the dictionaries. And far from being hot slang, it would seem to have been around for ages, at least in the US. *The Dictionary of American Regional English* has a citation from 1838, although with different spelling: 'Minard's talking & Peake's scribbling were enough to drive anyone ancey.'

This could be our current word. It would seem to mean 'mad' or 'crazy', but our 'antsy' is no more than 'agitated', 'restless' or 'impatient'.

'Antsy', with the modern spelling, is not recorded until the 1960s, when it appears almost simultaneously with 'antsy-pantsy'. Both are said to come from 'ants in the pants'. But that expression is not found before 1939, when the playwrights Kaufman and Hart used it in their comedy *The Man Who Came to Dinner*. If 'antsy' is really the much older dialect expression 'ancey', where did it spend the intervening 100 years?

The entomological word 'ant', by the way, comes from a Germanic term meaning 'a biter-off'. All of which makes 'ants in the pants' a powerful image, especially in Britain, where pants are a more intimate item of apparel than they are in the US.

The growing, but still infrequent use of 'antsy' on this side of the Atlantic led to its inclusion in the 1995 *Concise Oxford Dictionary*. That was followed, as is customary, by a storm of outrage about ephemeral Americanisms displacing useful British words. It's the kind of thing I have been known to get 'antsy' about myself. Whatever it means.

Asylum

'Asylum' is a word that has made a remarkable comeback. In the 1970s and 1980s, one of its principal meanings – a place for storing the mentally ill – had become taboo. Only a narrow, technical sense, associated with diplomacy, clung on: finding shelter in a foreign country or embassy when your own was out to get you.

Then the Berlin Wall came down, nations fell apart, and whole populations wanted to escape the chaos. When governments tried to stop what had always been called 'refugees', they came up against the Universal Declaration of Human Rights, agreed in 1948. It states that: 'Everyone has the right to seek, and to enjoy in other countries, asylum from persecution.' The 'asylum seeker' was born.

'Asylum' is a Latin word, adapted from the Greek *asulon*, meaning 'sanctuary'. At first, the English used a French variant, *asyle*. 'Asylum' itself arrived in the fifteenth century. Both words meant a place where those accused of crimes or bad debts sought religious protection.

By the seventeenth century, however, it had come to mean any place of refuge or the abstract idea of refuge itself. You didn't have to be mad to go there. That only came in with the eighteenth and nineteenth centuries, when the term was also used for homes for the blind, the incurable and the destitute.

'Lunatics' were renamed the mentally ill, and 'asylums' became hospitals. But the concept of 'asylum' lived on in international relations. If your own country is planning to prosecute you, you can ask for shelter – 'political asylum' – in some other country's embassy or in that country itself.

This is how a string of dissidents, deserters and spies came to be offered 'asylum' in the West during the Cold War. Their own countries wanted them, and so did we. The plight of the modern 'asylum seeker' is somewhat different.

Avatar

Avatar

Do you have an 'avatar'? You will soon.

Years ago, at a computer exhibition, I remember hearing that 'avatars' were the Next Big Thing. These were cartoon characters who would appear on your computer screen when you used the Internet and thus somehow 'represent' you in that Nowhere Land known as cyberspace.

Since my 'avatar' was a dog-headed nymphet in a purple jumpsuit, the notion was easy to resist. But the 'avatar' survives.

The word comes from Hinduism. The Sanskrit word *avatara* means 'descent' and an 'avatar' is a god who has descended to the earth and adopted a mortal form. Vishnu, for instance, is said to adopt ten forms, from a fish to a winged horse that will one day destroy the earth.

Occasionally, 'avatar' is used metaphorically, to indicate that someone or something embodies an idea. You might say, for instance, that Richard Branson is the avatar of enterprise, unless you use his trains.

But the computer world has adopted the term, to describe the descendants of my canine-featured alter ego. 'Avatars' may not always look like that nowadays, but they still profess to represent a user in negotiations with a computer network.

Thus a software 'avatar' might search out the cheapest CDs on the Net, send the cash, and arrange delivery. It might even choose a few more that it just knows I will love. All of which leaves me free for important tasks, like scraping the fluff from my mouse.

It seems I have become God, and the 'avatar' is my incarnation on earth. Unfortunately, I find myself reminded rather more of a homunculus or familiar spirit that I can't control.

'Such avatars ... are potentially dangerous,' agreed computer thinker Peter Small, in the publicity for his 1998 book *Magical A-Life Avatars*. 'They could catalyse a process which subjugates the human race to a new and sinister alien life form.'

Cripes! Come back, Vishnu, all is forgiven.

Balti

'Balti' is the dish that ate Britain, escaping from its Midlands stronghold and moving relentlessly across the country.

And a dish is exactly the word. For those who have not succumbed, 'balti' is a meat curry, cooked and served in a 'balti', a metal dish like a two-handled wok, and eaten with bread.

The roots of 'balti' are contentious. There is general agreement only that it was created in Birmingham at the start of the 1990s. According to *The Balti Bible*, it was introduced by a restaurateur from 'Baltistan', in the mountainous north of Pakistan. And 'balti' is also said to be an Urdu word for the utensil, usually known as a 'karai', favoured by the 'Baltis'.

This account does not convince some Indian chefs, who take a dim view of the whole phenomenon. In most Indian languages, they complain, 'balti' means nothing more than 'bucket'. Such an object has nothing to do with food. Some even insist that there was no such place as 'Baltistan'.

The *Encyclopaedia Britannica* recognizes it, but points out that the inhabitants of Baltistan 'eke out a meagre living growing crops'. Hardly the background for a hearty cuisine aimed at carnivorous Brummies.

An alternative explanation has been suggested. Fed up with their ignorant English customers, waiters in a Birmingham curry house amused themselves by concocting a dubious 'speciality' that they called 'balti', or 'the bucket'. Soon the customers started asking for it elsewhere, and chefs were happy to oblige.

Apparently, the style has some resemblance to the rugged fare of Peshawar and the North West Frontier. That's 1,500 miles away from the homeland of the Bengalis who cook 'balti', but geographically quite close to lofty Baltistan itself.

The kitchen is no place for purists. Who has not eaten Mexican food cooked by Glaswegians? The problem with 'balti' is that the word, which may originate from *balde*, the Portuguese for bucket, is more interesting than the food.

Bears v bulls

Where do 'bulls' tussle with 'bears' without incurring the wrath of the RSPCA? In the City of London, where they represent rising and falling share prices and those who stand to benefit from them.

'Bears' speculate on falling prices: they agree a price now for stock they expect to drop in value. Then they wait to buy it until the price has dropped (if it does), sell at the agreed high price and pocket the difference.

Originally the 'bear' – from the Old English *bera* and before that Teutonic – was the stock, rather than the person selling it. Indeed, it may once have been the 'bearskin', since in the City coffee houses of the early eighteenth century the seller was known as a 'bearskin jobber'.

Ultimately, it refers to a proverb: 'to sell the bear's skin before one has caught the bear'. 'Bears' always take that risk: they sell something they don't own, so they can get caught out.

A 'bull' – from the Middle English *bole*, apparently based on an early German verb meaning 'to roar' – is someone who speculates on a rising market, buying cheap and expecting (or helping) prices to rise. It, too, is first recorded in the early years of the eighteenth century, but there is no handy proverb to explain its origins. It seems simply to have arisen as an alliterative counterpart to 'bear'.

Neither term reflects particularly well on speculators. Bears are proverbially uncouth and bad-tempered. Bulls are reckless and impetuous. They also produce a great deal of 'bull', a military slang term for nonsense since World War I, with or without its crude suffix.

It is worth noting that both 'bear' and 'bull' emerged with the South Sea Bubble of 1720, a disastrous speculation in shares in unprofitable enterprises that promised, one day, to make vast fortunes. For some reason, this seems to ring a bell.

Belter

When a friend tells you that he had 'a belter' last night, should you congratulate, commiserate – or call an ambulance?

It rather depends who's speaking. In current slang, a 'belter' is an exciting or thrilling experience, so they obviously had a good time. On the other hand, in Scots and Lancashire dialects, a 'belter' can be 'a heavy blow, or series of blows'. You wouldn't want to get the two muddled up.

In the Teutonic of northern Europe in the Dark Ages, there was a word, probably derived from the Latin *balteum*, that would one day turn into 'belt'. It meant a strip of leather you wear around your waist. From medieval times, to 'belt' someone or something was to put a 'belt' around it, often as an honour: you 'belted' someone to make them a knight, for instance.

It would be unfair to suggest that the Puritan-era Scots invented the idea of hitting people, particularly children, with heavy leather accessories. Nonetheless, they were the first to use 'to belt' in that way, in 1649. From there it went around the world.

But where are the thrills and excitement? Well, sex and violence aren't only the staples of modern television. They are also the stuff of our language, with the unappealing result that both 'belt' and 'belter' have been used of sexually voracious women and prostitutes.

Luckily, there are more innocent associations. From Gloucestershire dialect, we acquired 'to belt', meaning to hurry or race along. The Prohibition-era Americans gave us 'to belt the bottle', meaning to drink heavily – or 'hit it hard'.

And then there is also 'to belt out' a song. A 'belter' in this sense is a singer who sacrifices subtlety, intelligence and communication in favour of sheer brassy attack. As the old joke has it, less *Bel Canto* than 'Can Belto': but a good recipe for a 'belter' of an evening.

Big

Here's a prominent pop musician of the 1990s explaining why his band had always favoured a particular DJ: 'He was always bigging us up.'

The verb 'to big', or 'to big up', is not standard English, but you can guess that it means to promote, to praise, to make 'big'. Here 'big' means successful, an American nuance first recorded in 1903.

No one knows where 'big' originally came from. It is first recorded in Northumbria at the end of the thirteenth century, suggesting it may be Norse. But the only similar Norse word means 'to dwell', giving us the word 'bigly', meaning habitable.

'Big' was first used of powerful people. Perhaps that was because they had 'bigly' houses? It also applied to fierce storms and battles, but nothing that was merely large. That only came in the fifteenth century.

In the nineteenth century, what we later called the 'Big Country' began to exert an influence. On the one hand, the Americans coined positive expressions like 'big of you', meaning magnanimous or noble, and epithets like 'the Big Apple', 'the big time', 'big league' and 'Big Mac'. On the other, they gave us 'big mouth' and 'big Government', both terms of abuse. Not to mention 'the Big C'.

'Big Brother' is our own. But before George Orwell he was quite well liked, lending his name to a 1920s movement intended to help boys emigrate to Australia *on their own*. In future, of course, Orwell's dictator will only appear in the footnotes of learned studies of an epoch-making television show.

And what of 'big up'? It is West Indian, picked up by white youths from Jamaican patois and dance-hall MCs, a development parodied in the funny but unsettling comedy character of 'Ali G'. To whom a 'big shout' goes out, at least for daring.

Bladdered

'I don't know what happened,' said the Cardiff accountant whose millennium night was so lively that he had to take out a newspaper advertisement to apologize. 'But you could say I was right royally bladdered.'

The phrase suggests a relish in the sheer sound of words reminiscent of his compatriot, Dylan Thomas; another man who knew all about the state described.

To be 'bladdered' is to be drunk. It's a piece of slang found no earlier than the early 1990s, at first among students and then more widely. You don't have to be Dr Jonathan Miller to work out why 'bladdered' should mean intoxicated. Intoxication has powerful effects on the urinary tract, especially the sort of intoxication that tends to follow a 'session' involving copious supplies of what marketing people call 'throwing lager'.

That alone, however, would not seem to explain the appeal of 'bladdered': it is not as if there is any shortage of synonyms and euphemisms for 'drunk'. But 'bladdered' has a nicely emphatic sound that lends itself to boasting about being drunk, an essential part of the experience, especially for the young. The sound is also reminiscent of earlier words associated with drunkenness: 'blotto' at the turn of the century, 'blind' or 'blinded' in the 1930s, 'blitzed' and 'plastered' in the 1940s and 1950s, and 'blasted' more recently. Even if you've never heard the term before, you can quickly grasp its meaning.

'Bladder' itself is found in the earliest Anglo-Saxon texts, and in all the Teutonic languages. 'A membranous bag in the animal body,' is the *OED*'s first definition. It has, over the years, had some amusing figurative meanings: a pompous windbag, a bald man and, in the US, a bad newspaper.

Newspapers made much of Mr Potter's apology, much to the annoyance of the Welsh branch of the Association of Chartered and Certified Accountants, which dropped him as official spokesman. Characters are all very well, but not in accountancy.

Blinding!

Recently I bought a copy of the *Big Issue*. The man took the money, and then, instead of the usual 'Cheers!' or even 'Thank you', he said 'Blinding!'

What did he mean? The *OED* is no help, unless the cheerful indigent was referring to 'the process of covering the surface of a newly made road with fine material to fill up the spaces between the stones', which seems unlikely. A good modern dictionary of slang will have it, though. Here's Jonathan Green's version: 'Wonderful, terrific, perfect, etc.'

When the *OED* catches up, 'Blinding (exclamation)' will take its place in a vast list of meanings arising from the word 'blind', starting with 'destitute of the sense of sight' and ending with 'blind-worm: a reptile also called a slow-worm' (which isn't blind at all, although unlikely to win any 'Miss Beautiful Eyes' contests).

This sheer linguistic bulk is a tribute to the age and stability of the word (virtually identical in Old English, Old Saxon and most languages with a Teutonic root), and to blindness's role as a source of figurative language.

Our enthusiastic 'blinding' obviously relates to a 'blinder', which is a 'dazzling' sporting feat. To dazzle is to overpower by strong light. Its effect is 'to deprive of sight temporarily', the *OED*'s very second meaning of 'to blind', the first being 'to deprive of sight permanently'.

We are often 'dazzled' by something 'brilliant', which would seem another simile for our homeless man's 'blinding'. But whereas a 'brilliant' book casts figurative light into our moral darkness, to 'blind' has always meant 'to close the eyes of the understanding or moral perception'.

A homeless person may find the change he gets for selling the *Big Issue*, or my generosity in buying it, 'blinding'. They may, however, be 'blinding' him to the realities of his predicament.

Blip

'Low inflation or nil inflation is a fact of life,' said a man from John Lewis, explaining static sales figures. 'It isn't a blip.'

But what *is* a 'blip'? There is a mental association between inflation and 'blips', but they are only linked for historical reasons. In 1988, Nigel Lawson, best known now as the father of a television cook but then Chancellor of the Exchequer, announced that a near-doubling of inflation in less than a year was 'a temporary blip'.

He was conjuring up a mental image of a line on a graph. The x or across axis shows time; the y or up axis shows prices. A gently rising line crosses the page. But suddenly there's a sharp upward spike. The Chancellor's description of this as a 'blip' indicated his confidence that it would drop equally sharply. We remember it because no one else shared his faith.

The word 'blip' has two elements, auditory and visual. In its earliest usages, it imitates the sound of a tap or blow. Mark Twain used it in 1895 for a blow: 'We took him a blip in the back and knocked him off.' It was a replacement, occasional only, for 'thump', 'bash' and 'bop'.

It only established itself in the 1940s, with the invention of radar. Here it was essentially visual. The cathode ray screens on the earliest radar sets showed a single horizontal line. The target would appear as a 'blip', a visible spike on that line, indicating its distance away. Later, when rotating aerials came in, the display was circular and 'blips' showed distance and direction.

The 'blip' mentioned by both Mr Lawson and the man from John Lewis is, then, a short-term 'spike' on an otherwise flat graph. But it is not a meaningless visual error. Although it is rarely conscious, anyone talking about a blip is making an analogy with radar. And on a radar screen, a 'blip' means trouble approaching, as Mr Lawson duly discovered.

Bobbins

If someone says 'It's bobbins,' try not to ask 'When will Bobbin be finished with it?'

Here's an actual example of the phrase in use. 'Let's be honest and say the referee was absolute bobbins,' declared the defeated football manager. 'If you need that translating, he was crap.'

We could probably have worked that out for ourselves. 'Bobbins' means rubbish, useless, or nonsense. It is a word associated with sport and pop music, but mostly with the natives of Manchester, who have done their best to spread it around the country, helped by their apparent stranglehold on the popular media. Take it from me, if you want to be on the television, stop those elocution lessons today.

But what makes 'bobbins' rubbish, or worse? A 'bobbin' is literally a reel to hold cotton or other thread. Sadly, this is one of those words whose origins remain a mystery: one of only 1,300 where the *OED* admits defeat. 'Bobbin' appeared fully formed, probably from the French, in the mid-sixteenth century.

Originally 'bobbins' were hand-made in wood or bone. In the nineteenth century, the word was applied to textile machinery, notably in the woollen mills, and to the disposable holders for the yarn. Such 'bobbins' were discarded when the wool they were holding came to an end. Hence, 'bobbins' = rubbish.

But while the mills are largely silent, 'bobbins' live on. In the electronics industry, they are the formers around which coils and transformers are wound. They are also a unit of currency in those peculiar local trading schemes where people barter their skills: you unblock my drains, I'll design you a website and we'll pay each other one 'bobbin' each.

In the world of antiques, meanwhile, pre-industrial 'bobbins' are highly prized. A lucrative trade has grown up in faking them, using animal bones dyed in manure. In other words, one thing that definitely isn't 'bobbins' is a bobbin.

Bogus

Bogus

Few words are more beloved of the more strident tabloids than 'bogus'. Every time a 'bogus asylum seeker' is found to have made a 'bogus benefit claim' their news editors must feel like Christmas has come early.

For years 'bogus' was a word we read in headlines but tended not to say, like 'quiz' or 'probe'. But its resurgence among the teenagers of America changed that, even if they used it to mean something quite different.

'Bogus' was born in the Wild West. Its first appearance in print, in 1827, was in the *Telegraph* of Painesville, Ohio, where it meant a machine for making counterfeit coins. As those 'boguses' turned out 'bogus money', the word had changed from noun to adjective. By the end of the nineteenth century, it had been imported to Britain, applied to anything false, spurious or deliberately misleading.

But in the 1960s, US computer scientists redefined it to mean 'non-functional', 'useless', or 'unbelievable', especially in relation to calculations and engineering ideas.

Emerging among Princeton and Yale graduates, it moved into the East Coast computer community, spinning off short-lived variants: 'bogosity', 'bogon', 'bogometer' and 'bogue out'. Eventually it was adopted by surfers, slackers and teenagers generally, simply to mean 'bad'. The *Bill and Ted* and *Wayne's World* movies spread it to the outside world.

The 1827 'bogus' machine seems to have been named by an onlooker at the time of its capture. The *OED* suggests a connection with a New England word, 'tantrabogus', perhaps related to the Dorset 'tantarabobs', meaning the devil.

A rival US account sees it as a corruption of the name of a forger, called Borghese, or Borges. Another idea connects it with the French word 'bagasse', meaning the refuse from sugar-cane production, which was used to make 'bogus', a dangerous drink.

There is a good word for these explanations: no doubt it will come to me.

Brainstorming

Be careful with 'brainstorming': it can be dangerous. Not the activity, but the word. Some people find it offensive, and want it banned.

How can that be? In 1894, when the science of neurology was some way short of its current precision, George M. Gould published his *Illustrated Dictionary of Medicine*. He coined the term 'brainstorm', defining it as 'a succession of sudden and severe phenomena, due to some cerebral disturbance'.

Pretty vague, but that made it a gift for lawyers, notably those representing Harry Thaw, the multimillionaire and wastrel at the centre of 1906's most celebrated murder. Thaw put three bullets into the head of New York architect Stanford White while he watched a musical. Thaw's lawyers blamed a 'brain storm' and he was acquitted on appeal.

Thaw's cerebral meteorology was temporarily as famous as O.J. Simpson's gloves. 'Brainstorm' entered American slang, but oddly it meant a sudden good idea. Our 'brainwave', meanwhile, is from mysticism rather than medicine.

The pseudo-medical 'brainstorm' can be found as late as 1922 in the *Daily Mail* – and not only in the readers' letters. But Norman Hunter's wonderful Professor Branestawm, created in 1933, is a man whose mental flashes are essentially creative.

It was in 1939 that American advertising man Alex Osborn invented 'the brain storm session', the central ritual of the flipchart folk. Everyone calls out ideas, without let or hindrance, and someone writes them up on a board or a big pad.

So where's the harm? 'Brain', Old English for the blob of natural yoghurt between your ears, meets 'storm', Old English for a violent burst of weather. It has no more connection with real neurological or psychological disorder than 'heartburn' has with cardiology.

In its country of origin, 'brainstorming' upsets no one. Even neurological patients 'brainstorm' as part of their therapy.

Over here, however, the Technique Formerly Known As Brainstorming has a new name. We are supposed to call it 'cloudbursting'. How wet.

Brassy

Early in his period as Conservative leader, William Hague took the time to explain to us what it means to be British. His speech contained 6,800 words, some heading dangerously towards the thoughtful.

But one jarred. Mr Hague wanted Britain to be 'urban, ambitious, sporty, fashion-conscious, multi-ethnic, brassy, self-confident and international'.

What was 'brassy' doing there? Certainly it's a word made for his 'muck 'n' brass' Yorkshire vowels, while being equally reminiscent of that Lancastrian stereotype, Bet Lynch, in whose person 'brassy' was eternally coupled with 'blonde', 'busty' and 'barmaid'.

But in tabloid language, 'brassy' people are noisy, like brass instruments, and vulgar, like brass ornaments. They are from the old pre-Thatcherite North. They are neither sporty, multi-ethnic nor international.

And that's as good as 'brassy' gets. Otherwise, this is a word with a nasty metallic taste. In Anglo-Saxon times, brass was what we call bronze. Later it came to mean the modern alloy of copper and zinc, used for plaques in churches, musical instruments, and money.

Things made from 'brass' are 'brazen'. And because 'brazen' objects are hard and flashy, the word came to mean 'impudent' or 'shameless'. 'Brass' and 'brassy' soon acquired the same connotations. 'You have the brass to . . .' and 'bold as brass' were both with us before the French Revolution.

Shakespeare uses 'brassy' to mean hard, merciless or cruel, but it also meant pushy or forward, the same as 'brazen'. Unflattering comparisons were made between 'our brassy age' and the 'Golden Age'. It also meant hard, strident and unsubtle, qualities associated with brass instruments, especially if you stand near one.

Applied to women, 'brassy' is hardly a compliment. It means flashy, ostentatious and hard. And a 'brass' is a prostitute. 'Brass' is short for 'brass nail', rhyming slang for 'tail'. And 'tail' is . . . Well, you can probably guess what 'tail' is.

A 'brassy' Britain, Mr Hague? No thanks.

Broker

The Internet makes everything more complicated, especially if you want to work in it. Fancy 'leveraging existing contacts in the publishing world to broker new content transactions' to quote a recent job advertisement? Possibly, but what does it mean?

It means commissioning words and pictures from journalists. Being a website's editor, in other words, although that function is normally exercised by one of the designers in the lunch break.

To the young and excitable, words such as 'broker' and 'leveraging' are redolent of money and power, with a whiff of Wall Street.

The word 'broker' hardly deserves such respect. Derived from various French and Anglo-French words, it seems originally to have meant someone who sells drink *au broc* or 'on tap'. Small beer, then. By the time of Langland's *Piers Plowman*, at the end of the fourteenth century, it was an unflattering term for someone selling second-hand furniture.

Two centuries later, Ben Jonson was even less enthusiastic: in *Every Man in His Humour* he refers to 'a broker, one of the devil's own kinsmen'. Did I mention that a 'broker' was also a synonym for pimp, procurer, bawd or pander, as recently as the early eighteenth century? Or that in Dickens, a 'broker' sells the chattels of families evicted for non-payment of rent?

But then 'brokers' became respectable. In the nineteenth century, the term applied to those selling the output of Britain's mills and factories. Later it became the Stock Exchange term for someone who buys and sells shares on behalf of the public, as opposed to a 'jobber', who trades on his own account.

Both jobs have been replaced by the 'broker-dealer', who works for a 'securities house'. Nonetheless, 'brokers' of various sorts are as active as ever. They have recently acquired an American verb, 'to broker', with which to glorify themselves and irritate the rest of us.

That leaves the old 'to broke', still used in the 1960s, surplus to requirements. Any offers?

Bug

He's got the model railway 'bug'. She's found a new 'bug' in her computer. The kids want to dig up 'bugs'. I think I'm going down with a 'bug'.

'Bug' is a little word with lots of meanings. The use of 'bug' for an insect sounds American to most British ears, but it was an English term, used especially for beetles and bedbugs, as long ago as the seventeenth century. Then it went to sleep and woke up on the other side of the Atlantic where the sheer profusion of insects provided better career prospects.

This 'bug' may simply be a descendant of *budde*, an older word for insect. More appealingly, it is the Welsh *bwg*, meaning a malevolent ghost or hobgoblin. Shakespeare is full of such 'bugs', which Johnson's dictionary defines as 'a walking spectre'.

No wonder 'bug' came to represent the creepy side of insect life. Later it came to mean the micro-organisms we often visualize as little insects: bacteria, viruses, prions, etc.

A person whose 'bug' is an enthusiasm, meanwhile, is in the tradition of the 'fire-bug': literally an American insect, the word later came to mean a pyromaniac, before being applied to milder crazes.

But the 'bug' in your computer has nothing directly to do with germs or insects. There is, in the Smithsonian museum, a dead moth, found inside an experimental computer in 1945. It was labelled at the time: 'first actual case of bug being found'. So the expression was already known. Indeed, it was used by Thomas Edison in 1889, when his prototype phonograph failed, and may have come from the telegraph industry.

Edison's 'bug' was imaginary, just like the imaginary 'gremlins' later invented by early RAF crews. History's most notorious imaginary 'bug' may yet prove to be the 'millennium' variety which, you will recall, was scary for a while – but totally harmless.

Busk

'I don't know anything about the subject,' confides the lecturer, 'but I'm going to busk it.' In the same way, a minister can 'busk' his way through parliamentary questions.

The implication is that a confidence trick is being perpetrated. But what has that to do with standing in Covent Garden, strumming a five-stringed guitar and singing 'Mull of Kintyre'?

The answer is that our 'busking' refers to a different musical practice. Among indoor musicians, to 'busk' is not to stand next to an upturned hat; it means to improvise from basic instructions rather than reading the music. It's not an inferior skill – quite the opposite in many ways – nor is it disreputable.

Nonetheless, outside that narrow field, 'busking' retains its dubious reputation. Which becomes less surprising when you know the associations of the word before it became musical terminology.

It started as the French *busquer*, which once meant to sneak around for the purposes of hunting or stealing. When 'to busk' appeared here, in the seventeenth century, it referred to the uncertain movement of ships, tacking in and out of the wind. By extension, it became possible for a person to go 'busking after one thing or another'.

But it found a lasting role in the slang of nineteenth-century London, where to 'busk' was to go round from pub to pub scratching a living. You'd do this by selling rude song sheets, drawing caricatures and, if all else failed, singing. The idea of 'busking' as open-air music came with the Edwardian seaside, at the turn of the twentieth century.

'Buskers' tend to prefer 'street performer', since 'busking' has in the past been taken as synonymous with vagrancy. But they needn't be defensive. Like improvising a musical part, teaching without preparation, or making a convincing Commons statement on something you know nothing about, street 'busking' is a lot harder than it looks. Even playing 'Mull of Kintyre'.

Candy

A piece of 'eye-candy' becomes the 'arm-candy' of someone in the 'mind-candy' business. Bored, she spends her days listening to 'ear-candy' and her nights taking 'nose-candy'.

Not much of a plot, even translated into English: 'An attractive woman becomes the consort of a television mogul who specializes in trivia. She listens to vacuous pop music and takes cocaine.'

But she doesn't eat sweets. The compounds here have nothing to do with eating. Instead 'candy' stands for anything sweet, alluring, instantly gratifying and either worthless or positively destructive.

Our 'sweets', which appeared in the eighteenth century as 'sweeties', won't work in this way. The word is plural where we need a singular, and it lacks transatlantic glamour. 'Candy' stars in pop songs and movies; 'sweets' live at the shop in *Coronation Street*.

The English had 'candy' first, actually, but we lost interest and left it on the bedpost of history. First there was 'sugar-candy', which began as a medieval Latin approximation of two Arabic words, *sukkar* and *qandi*.

Sukkar meant sugar, and so did *qandi*, which is derived from a word meaning 'broken'. Broken sugar, in other words, which is one way of describing the crystallization process that produces sugar-candy.

Variants on the Arabic are found in most of the medieval European languages. It arrived in England in the fourteenth century. As well as being used literally, 'sugar-candy' was a byword for anything pleasing in Elizabethan times and at intervals since.

'Candy' on its own, however, has rarely been used here since the eighteenth century, except in describing colours and stripes. But in America it became the standard term.

Its first sexual connotations arrived in the mid-nineteenth century. 'Nose-candy' arrived in the 1920s. But the modern vogue for '-candy' compounds follows 'ear-candy', defined by the *Merriam-Webster Dictionary* as 'music that is pleasing to listen to but that lacks depth'.

The expression appeared first in 1977, the year of the Sex Pistols. Presumably the person who coined it was thinking of someone else.

Cascade

Cascade

The City of London has a reputation for language. But what shocked some new recruits to banking was when they were told to 'cascade' their contributions to meetings.

A 'cascade' is literally a waterfall, from the Italian *cascata*, a fall. But it has come to stand for innumerable decidedly dry things in scientific, technical and business life.

In the 1980s, to 'cascade' information was to control it, feeding it in at the top of an organization and letting it run down. That was, of course, the heyday of 'trickledown' economics, borrowed by Ronald Reagan and Margaret Thatcher from Herbert Hoover, in which money was supposed to follow water's gravitational direction.

But this 'cascading' was not adopted directly from gazing at waterfalls and garden fountains. Since the 1930s, the verb has been extensively used in electrical and electronic engineering. Two or more components are 'cascaded' if they are connected to operate sequentially. And the verb has found an even more unlikely niche in the public-transport industry, where ancient trains or buses transferred to less demanding duty – for instance, serving London's commuters – are said to have been 'cascaded'.

Today, however, to 'cascade' information tends to mean to spit it out in small bursts. The analogy comes from the world of computers, in which the verb relates to everything from the way a program is written to the way web pages appear.

Most common is the idea of 'cascading windows'. This means windows arranged one behind another on the PC screen, each containing a small amount of information. You can see why clicking through them would be a neat analogy for the correct way to present information in an office context, even if it is only gossip.

City malcontents, averse to being tutored on how to speak in meetings, may, however, like to know that in the eighteenth and nineteenth centuries 'to cascade' meant 'to vomit'.

Champion

One minute they were civil servants, the next they were 'Information Age Government Champions'. They didn't even win anything.

'Champion' is a corporate buzzword. Here's the government's explanation: 'The group comprises 36 senior government officials at board level within departments who have been designated to champion the information age government agenda within their departments and agencies.' So that's clear.

These 'champions' are not alone. Britain's architects recently declared that towns should appoint 'civic champions' to promote the cause of good building. And the AA now advertises itself on television as 'your insurance champion'.

The reference is not to modern sport, in which someone becomes a 'champion' by defeating all comers, but to something older. These 'champions', civil servants or not, are gladiators.

The word comes from *campio*, Latin for someone who fights in the *campus* or arena. Arriving here in the thirteenth century, it was applied especially to a fighter who takes on someone else's cause, either for money or because he believes in it. In the Bible, Goliath is the 'champion' of the Philistines. It doesn't mean he won a series of heats before clashing with the unfancied David in the regional finals.

Our 'champions' claim to be taking up the cause of 'the information age government agenda' – whatever that is – civic design and the insurance purchaser respectively. It's an archaic use of the word. Since the eighteenth century, most of us have used 'champion' in the context of sporting competition. Are those who use 'champion' merely trading on that glory?

Most likely, they are trying to be like the Americans. In 1987, management gurus Tom Peters and Robert Waterman produced *In Search of Excellence*, which praised companies that encouraged 'champions': influential individuals who pushed projects through.

Since then, ambitious organizations have duly appointed their own 'champions'. Having a lot of 'champions', however, is not necessarily a recipe for winning anything.

Cheesy

If 'cheesy' means naff or tacky or unconvincing, why do we call the boss 'the Big Cheese'?

Take 'cheesy' first. A look through the newspapers sees this adjective applied to all sorts of people and things: novelty records, inept soap operas, the suits worn by computer dealers, the grins worn by some of our most famously grinning politicians.

It's an American expression, defined as shoddy, insubstantial and cheap. But before all that, of course, it meant 'pertaining to cheese' or 'resembling cheese'. As it still does – with less justice – on snack packaging.

The word 'cheese' is found in the earliest Anglo-Saxon texts, coming from the Latin *caseus* via Germanic. In 1,500 years, 'cheese' has not usually had negative associations. True, it smells. But before refrigeration it smelled a good deal worse, a good deal quicker. Yet 'cheesy' has only recently become a term of abuse.

It is actually recorded as 'a vague term of depreciation' among American students as early as 1896. Thereafter, it pops up throughout the century, even appearing in a W.H. Auden poem of 1951. But its vogue came in the 1980s on US campuses, where the fragrant comestible had long been associated with all manner of bodily functions and by-products.

But that is not the whole picture. In early and mid-nineteenth-century Britain, 'the cheese' meant 'the very best', or 'the right thing'. Sadly for cheese lovers, however, this has nothing to do with dairy produce. It comes from the Urdu or Persian *chiz*, meaning 'thing'. Hence, 'the real chiz' and then 'the real cheese'.

From this, too, comes 'The Big Cheese' and 'The Cheese', a 100-year-old expression that lives on. The modern alternative, 'honcho', is simply the Japanese *han'cho* (group leader), acquired by the Americans during World War II.

Despite the spelling, 'honcho' is nothing to do with the Spanish 'poncho'. That's the kind of assumption that can leave people 'cheesed off': a wartime expression now largely replaced by something ruder.

Childfree

When a word is new or controversial, it is often printed inside inverted commas. These 'scare quotes' warn readers to be on their guard. Then they quietly disappear.

Recently the word 'childfree' has emerged, passed through the 'scare quotes', and become acceptable in less than ten years. Which is odd if you consider that we already have a word for the condition of having no children.

But 'childfree', c. 1979, is a 'positive' way of describing that condition, whereas 'childless', c. 1200 AD, seems to contain a note of regret that some people reject.

Whereas the '-less' suffix comes from Old English, and gives us about 1,600 words in English, '-free' is rarely found before this century. There are only thirty-five examples in the *OED*, although it has yet to catch up with 'alcohol-free', 'lead-free', and 'cholesterol-free'.

Do they have implications beyond their literal meanings? Does the '-less' in 'childless' suggest a sad 'loss' of some good quality? You might think so, from 'heartless', 'loveless', 'bloodless', 'gutless', 'faithless' and many more. 'Childless' itself belongs in a family that includes 'motherless' and 'fatherless'. But '-less' does not always express an unhappy loss: consider 'painless', 'ageless' and 'tireless'.

What we can say is that the 1,000-year-old '-less' suffix tends to deal with the fundamentals of life before antiseptics and low-fat spreads. It was almost unknown before the 1920s, when 'germ-free', 'dust-free' and 'sugar-free' started to appear. These scientific terms were taken up in advertising, where people in white coats are still trusted.

'Childfree' is an invented term, created by an American movement of the same name which thinks the childless are supporting children: they seem to have forgotten that in old age they will depend upon that situation reversing.

The '-free' suffix is almost invariably associated with pests, dangers and health hazards. Children may sometimes fall into that category, but a term which sees them *only* as that betrays an unusual outlook.

Civilian

A message comes over the school tannoy: 'Civilian on the premises.' But before the full panoply of security can come into effect, the mystery is solved. It turns out to be a lost parent.

This wonderfully self-aggrandizing expression is so new that it features in no dictionaries. It has the benefit of suggesting that 'we', whether we be teachers, railway workers or journalists, are an élite corps of highly trained professionals, while everyone else is riff-raff.

There are, of course, situations in which it can be used quite legitimately: in the military, naturally, but also in the police and other uniformed services, who sometimes need to make a distinction between themselves and the 'civilians' they work alongside. Perhaps other trades picked it up from police series on television.

In origin, interestingly, 'civilian' has nothing to do with the military life. It is an adaptation of the Old French *civilien*, meaning anything connected with civil law. A 'civilian' was thus someone who taught or studied that type of law, as opposed to canon law. It appears in the prologue to the Wycliffe Bible of 1388: 'Sumtyme cyvylians and canonistris weren devout and . . . busy in her lernyng.'

Later, there was an interesting theological use. A 'civilian' was someone who rejected Christ but at the same time maintained a high standard of life. The standard modern use, meaning someone outside the military life, arrived only later, much to the horror of Thomas De Quincey, writing in the early nineteenth century, who decried 'The fashionable and most childish use of this word now current, – viz to indicate simply a non-military person – a use which has disturbed and perplexed all our past literature for six centuries.'

According to Partridge's *Dictionary of Slang*, though, the word was commonly used in the nineteenth century by criminals, to indicate anyone who was not one of their number. Our new idiom comes uncomfortably close to that.

Closure

Twice in a week, I find myself discussing 'closure'. Someone has left a job, but can't forget it: he hasn't achieved 'closure'. Someone else is writing a painful autobiographical book: he has an ending in mind, but will it provide the appropriate 'closure'?

In the language of therapy, 'closure' – meaning 'cutting off' or 'drawing a line' – is the precondition for 'moving on'. But are my friends, every one an uptight Englishman, really delving into the lexicon of Letting It All Out? Sure thing, as Oprah might say.

There could be other explanations. 'Closure' is also the rule in cricket that allows a captain to 'declare' when he is a long way ahead. But few Englishmen would know about that.

In Parliament, 'closure' is a vote to end a debate. And in phonetics, a 'closure' is when the mouth or throat moves to restrict the flow of air and hence sound. All very interesting, but nothing to do with the way we use the word now.

Turn instead to Gestalt psychology, founded in Germany before World War I and concerned with perception. These scientists considered the way patterns and shapes completed themselves in an onlooker's mind and called that 'closure'.

Thirty years later, Fritz S. Perls used the vocabulary of Gestalt psychology in founding Gestalt *psychotherapy*, which described the patterns and shapes in people's lives. Unlike the Freudians, Perls felt people should draw a line under the past rather than dwelling on it. For this, he borrowed the word 'closure'.

German by birth, Perls built his Gestalt movement in Esalen, California, during the 1960s. From the stormy Pacific Ocean to wild Rikki Lake is no distance at all.

The odd thing is that 'closure', which arrived here in the fourteenth century from French, did not originally mean shutting off or locking away, but locking in. Think on that, therapy fans.

Community

The word 'community' gets people going. 'The "homosexual community",' they snort, 'what kind of a community is that?' Others will insist that to call merchant bankers 'the finance community', or spies 'the intelligence community', is a nasty modern affectation.

In fact, it is 200 years old. In 1797, the radical William Godwin remarked that 'the literary world is an immense community'. In 1856, Ralph Waldo Emerson talked about 'the commercial community'. The 'Dutch community', the 'Jewish community' and the rest soon followed. Recently we have seen the 'surfing community' and the 'Linux community', who share a devotion to a type of computer software.

In medieval English, 'community' meant 'the common people', or members of a single state or political body. John Wycliffe used it in the 1380s.

It came from the Latin *communitatem*, and there it had meant 'joint ownership'. In sixteenth-century England, that sense was revived in denunciations of sects who tried 'community of wives' and 'community of goods', two social experiments more denounced than actually practised.

Over the years the groups covered by the word have stretched to include people in the same neighbourhood, religious and monastic bodies, the public as a whole and even groups of nations, for instance, the European Community.

Recently it has spawned compounds designed to soften old-fashioned paternalism, from 'community architecture' to 'community health'. For a while, Mrs Thatcher's 'community charge' – she alone actually called it that – rendered it unusable in political circles. But it sometimes crops up among Liberals and the kind of Labour MP who reserves the word 'socialism' for frightening the children.

Some traditional uses remain. There is, for instance, 'community singing', a great sporting ritual in which a man with a microphone sings 'Abide With Me' and the rest of the crowd sings 'Come on, you Reds' and 'You're gonna get your ****ing heads kicked in.' This is what we call 'community spirit'.

Cookin'

Cookin'

All it takes to kill a piece of youth slang is for some authority figure to adopt it. Which is why 'cookin'' couldn't survive the announcement by Mark Fisher, creative director of millennium night at the Dome, that the National Anthem would be turned into a 'cookin' piece of music' for the occasion.

Until then, this term of approval had been heard in all the right places: among dance musicians and DJs, revered jazz artists and American sports stars.

Of course, it was nothing new. It was first heard in the language of black American jazz as early as the 1940s. Bands that were 'hot' – back when 'hot' was better than 'cool' – were said to be 'cooking'.

'Cooking' – usually rendered 'cookin'' in imitation of the supposed speech patterns of those who coined it – was followed by more exotic variants, from 'Now we're cooking with gas' (or 'with electricity', or 'with radar') to 'We're cooking on both burners' (or 'on all four' or 'on the front burner').

All heard in the American club scene of the time, but better remembered here in tweedy British imitations: they crop up in the sort of film in which Kenneth More drops his pipe in astonishment when his date unexpectedly proves to be a demon jazz trumpeter.

Despite that, 'cooking' and its variants resurfaced in the 1990s, often in reference to music, but sometimes in more sober contexts. Teams of accountants, triumphing in some particularly testing audit, have been known to declare themselves 'cooking with gas'.

The verb 'to cook' came after the job title: it was what the 'cook' did. We had the noun from the turn of the first millennium, taken from the late Latin *cocus*.

Slang arrived later: to 'cook up' or falsify something, notably 'the books', arrived in the eighteenth century. To 'cook someone's goose' is nineteenth century. But as an expression of contemporary youth, 'cookin'' is about as relevant as the National Anthem.

Cop

'Cop a look at that,' says your companion, swivelling round on his bar stool to indicate some attractive arrival. 'Not much cop,' you say. 'Cop hold of this,' he says, asking you to hold his coat. Soon he's 'copped off', so you 'cop out'.

These are busy times for the modern 'cop'. It is ubiquitous among the young, for whom it readily replaces 'get' or 'take'. But beyond that it has a whole range of meanings from as far afield as Australia and North America.

In sixteenth-century Scotland and the North, the word 'cap' (from the Old French *caper*, to seize) meant 'arrest': 'Cap him, sir!' By the eighteenth century this had transformed itself into 'cop'. Soon it was slang for 'policeman'. 'To cop it' was to be reprimanded. Only in the twentieth century did it start to mean 'to be killed'.

In the nineteenth century, at least according to newspapers, criminals really did say 'It's a fair cop' when they were picked up. In contrast, something that was 'no cop' or 'not much cop' was a bad arrest, not worth all the paperwork, and hence a useless thing.

To 'cop out' is American, from the beatnik era, It means to give up: for instance, going home to your parents rather than sitting in a flat growing a beard and learning to play the bongos.

The ubiquitous 'cop a look' is said to be Australian, from the 1930s, now spread abroad by the dramatic feast that is *Neighbours*. 'To cop hold of', meanwhile, is British: as well as 'arrest', 'cop' always meant to 'catch' in northern dialect.

'Cop' has any number of sexual connotations in American slang, but 'cop off', meaning to 'get off with someone', is northern English. The word 'cop' is recorded in dialect as meaning everything from 'to behave saucily' to 'to grab hold of', which would seem to cover most of the activities associated with the expression.

Creative

These days, 'creative' is the thing to be. Even so, it's a surprise to see this notice in Sainsbury's: 'The creative desserts have moved to aisle 19, near the jellies.' Perhaps they are sitting there doing a bit of water-colouring, or penning a few lines of verse?

Close investigation of aisle 19 reveals that 'creative' desserts are not blancmanges with an aptitude for original invention but cake mixes, packet whips and the like, requiring the addition of water, milk and so on. In other words, the desserts are not 'creative' at all: that's the province of the cook (if that's not too rarefied a term).

On the face of it, then, a misuse of the word. 'Having the quality of creating, given to creating' is the *OED*'s first definition. In its early days the word – from the Latin verb *creare*, to produce – tended to be reserved for the Creator, or for godlike artists, rather than for supermarket puddings.

A moment's thought, however, makes it clear that Sainsbury's use is legitimate, if slightly idiosyncratic. Since the turn of the last century, people have used 'creative' to mean 'made by imagination' in the context of 'creative writing' and 'creative art'.

Creativity has, however, been devalued over the years. We have had 'creative play', and 'creative education' and, in the 1970s, 'creative accountancy'. Once an American term of abuse for the imaginative interpretation of a company's books, this is now, apparently, a legitimate practice.

Every year new arts graduates comb the 'Creative & Media' pages of the *Guardian* for a 'creative job': but they should beware. As the advertisements indicate, in modern management parlance it's possible to be a 'creative salesman', a 'creative admin assistant' or a 'creative food retail manager'.

Their creativity may not be of a sort Wordsworth would have recognized, but who can deny that it takes real ingenuity to package a sachet full of milk powder, sweeteners and colour as a feat of culinary artistry?

Cushty

If you are buying a car, according to one of the television pundits, everything needs to be 'cushty'. Or possibly 'cushti', 'cushdy' or 'kushti'.

It's not a word you often see written down, existing mainly in the speech of children and the young. But now it has turned up in the mouth of a middle-aged television presenter in a sports jacket, we will have to agree on a spelling.

'Cushty' – as good as any – means fine, great or excellent. It sounds like a relative of the older 'cushy', but with a slightly different meaning. A 'cushy' job is comfortable, soft and easy, but not necessarily good. That adjective appeared at the start of the twentieth century, and is particularly associated with World War I. That was when we learned of the 'cushy wound': an injury sufficiently danger-ous to send you home but not to kill you.

Given its pronunciation and meaning, it would seem natural to connect 'cushy' with 'cushion', a byword for easy living since the fourteenth century. As it happens, there was briefly a word 'cushiony', meaning exactly the same as 'cushy', which appeared at around the same time.

But most derive 'cushy' from sources further afield. It is said to be Anglo-Indian, picked up by soldiers during the Raj and derived from the Hindustani *khush*, meaning pleasant. Another even more exotic source is sometimes mentioned: the Romany (or Romani) *kushto*, apparently meaning good. But that is actually a lot closer to 'cushty'.

Either way, the ultimate source of both words would seem to be the Indian subcontinent. Modern kids, though, have picked up 'cushty' from British television. It was used in the 1980s sitcom *Only Fools and Horses*, which some say reflects its real use in the occupa-tional dialect of wide boys and dodgy dealers generally.

And now here it is being used by a television presenter in the context of the used-car trade. What an extraordinary coincidence.

Ditsy

The best way of defining 'ditsy' is to list the characters to whom it is applied: Ally McBeal, the world's least likely lawyer; the blonde girl in the Philadelphia cheese adverts; and anyone played by Meg Ryan. Meryl Streep, on the other hand, is rarely included.

'Ditsy', according to the *Merriam-Webster Collegiate Dictionary*, means 'eccentrically silly, giddy or inane'. But when it first appeared, in the late 1970s, it had a different definition. It was a fashion term, meaning fussy or intricate.

Frank Rich, the notorious *New York Times* theatre critic, was one of those who took it up in the 1980s, applying it in an unflattering way to the feather-brained female characters he saw onstage. It arrived in Britain, *c.* 1989, via the arts pages.

The *OED* suggests that the original fussy 'ditsy' was really 'dicty', a black American term from the Jazz Age, meaning 'posh' or 'conceited'. But the two words sound quite dissimilar and inhabit different worlds.

Most see 'ditsy' (sometimes spelt 'ditzy') as a simple modification of 'dizzy'. That seems entirely plausible, especially given its origins in a country where, thanks to the Italian influence, 'zz' is quite naturally assumed to be pronounced 'ts'.

In the US, the word 'dizzy' has long indicated that someone was mentally or morally shaky. The 'dizzy blonde', surely the great-grandmother of today's 'ditsy blonde' with her fistful of soft cheese, emerged there in the 1880s.

We, on the other hand, have generally used 'dizzy' to mean 'giddy', physically unbalanced. But it wasn't always the case. From Anglo-Saxon times to the end of the thirteenth century, *dusie* or 'dizzy' meant 'foolish', a meaning it retained in dialect. Many quintessential American expressions are essentially English dialect words that emigrated.

In Old English, however, a *dusie* was usually a man. The misogynistic streak in 'ditsy' (and 'ditz', the unlovely noun derived from it) is an American invention.

Dotcom

Having terrorized industry and turned business economics upside down, 'dotcom' has found a new role – as a colour of paint.

Normally, an appearance on a Dulux paint chart would indicate that a word's days at the cutting edge were over. But 'dotcom' is still busy, meaning 'a company that operates primarily via the Internet'. It would be nice, though, to agree on its spelling.

Some still favour 'dot.com'. But as pedants note, the dot is pronounced, so 'dot.com' is really 'dot-dot-com'. The simpler form makes sense.

To the Anglo-Saxons, a *dott* was 'the head of a boil'. By the eighteenth century, it had come to include any small mark made by a pen, including those above 'i' and 'j'. The 'dot' at the end of a sentence, however, was a full stop, a full point or, in the US, a period.

In many computer languages, a stop is used to separate the name of a document from its type. But it was traditionally silent: 'dodgy.doc' is pronounced 'dodgy doc'. In the 1970s, the stops turned up in Internet addresses, a string of numbers separated by 'periods': 192.197.62.35. This was called 'dot notation' and the things themselves referred to as 'dots'.

In the early 1990s, words were incorporated into Internet addresses so that human beings could read them, but the dots lived on. Commercial organizations were awarded addresses ending in .com: for instance, 'Amazon.com'. Speakers of 'Commonwealth' English pronounced the dot, and for once everyone followed.

For a while, a 'dotcom' was just a commercial Internet address. But then it became trendy. A 'DotCom' cafe opened in Toronto. There were even geek jokes, featuring programmers with children called Dotcom, Mozilla and Eudora.

By 1998, though, the current meaning had triumphed. Investors wanted 'dotcoms', Internet-based businesses, or they wanted old firms to 'dotcom' themselves. A lot of excitement for a tin of Dulux emulsion to express: what a pity it's a kind of grey.

Down

'The system's gone down,' you tell the man from the computer department. 'That's down to the way you're using it,' he suggests. 'Well, it's down to you to fix it,' you respond.

If ever a word was on the up, it's the adverb 'down'. The last few years have seen it occupying all sorts of new territory.

Everyone knows that while computers never go wrong, they do 'go down' an awful lot. 'Down to the way you're using it' means 'can be blamed on' your approach. But when you say it's 'down to you to fix it', you actually mean it's 'your job'.

'Down' began as a noun meaning a hill: it survives in numerous place names. As *dun*, it can be found in Anglo-Saxon texts from the seventh century. It may even be Celtic, given the appearance of similar syllables in Welsh and Roman British place names.

Our adverb 'down' derives from 'adown', the Old English *adune*, meaning 'off the hill'. 'Down' usually expresses a descent. If you 'come down' with a disease, you drop from vertical to horizontal.

Can equipment come 'down' with a bug? The *OED* has this amusing reference to the high technology of the 1760s: 'She happened to look at her watch, but it was down.' But clocks, steam engines, lathes and knitting machines don't go 'down'. They go wrong.

No computers went 'down' before about 1965. But 'downtime' had arrived in the early 1950s, when computers were unknown. 'Downtime' was when workers 'downed tools' because their machinery was not working. When computers caused 'downtime', were they said to be 'down'?

Meanwhile, the computer man's 'down to' is just a shortened version of a much older idiom. He is really saying it can be 'put down in writing in a book and held against you'. And 'down to you' is just 'up to you', a poker term introduced from the States in the early 1900s. The expression turned upside down in the 1970s for no good reason. But that goes for a lot of things.

Ecstasy

Ecstasy

How sad to think that a whole generation only knows 'ecstasy' as a drug. It's more interesting than that.

'Ecstasy' is a symptom, a mental state provoked by anything from religion to sport. The word is the Greek *ekstasis*, usually translated as 'a displacement' or 'a putting out of place'. The thing displaced, traditionally, is the soul, which leaves the body. 'Out of it,' as the drug enthusiasts say.

The Greeks used the word for everything from stark insanity to mild bewilderment. In New Testament Greek, it describes people's reactions to miracles. In the King James version this becomes 'great astonishment' and 'wonder and amazement'. But the same Greek word also describes the state the apostles entered when praying, and here the translation is 'trance'.

In English, 'ecstasy' had already been used, in John Wycliffe's fourteenth-century Bible. His habit was to use the Greek words and paraphrase them. Thus his apostles experience 'extasie, that is, leesing of mynde of resoun and lettyng of tunge'. Releasing the mind from reason and loosening the tongue: a typical Saturday night in some parts.

Early writers in English used it for both great disturbance and a kind of catalepsy. Macbeth tosses and turns 'in restless ecstasie'; but when the enraged Othello 'falls in a trance', to quote the stage direction, that is described by Iago as 'your ecstasy'.

Mystical and medical writers concentrated on the trance. 'Ecstasy' became a mental state or religious vision so intense that bodily sensation ceased. It was terrifying: only after being abused by poets as an analogy for literary inspiration did 'ecstasy' come to mean pleasure or joy.

Interestingly, drugs and 'ecstasy' were linked long before the arrival, in 1985, of MDMA, a synthetic pharmaceutical lacking a snappy street name. In 1969, for instance, an earlier drug guru, Timothy Leary, published *The Politics of Ecstasy*, his psychedelic manifesto. Forgotten now, as 'Ecstasy' will one day be. But 'ecstasy' will carry on for ever.

Eggy

'Don't get all eggy,' says one nine-year-old to another. But this is a playground dispute, not a cookery lesson. What's going on?

Context tells us that 'eggy' means 'annoyed'. Children in these parts say it all the time, but perhaps it's a local thing. You rarely see it written down, although it has been heard on live television and radio, and not just Radio Gloucestershire.

According to most dictionaries, 'eggy' means 'egg-like' or 'full of egg': 'the sponge cake was moist and eggy', and so on. No surprises there. The word 'egg' has its origins in Common Teutonic and took its present form in English in about the fifteenth century.

Luckily, the *OED* has a second definition for 'eggy': 'annoyed, irritated', which it describes as *colloq* and *dial*. It cites something called *Lern Yerself Scouse*, from 1966. But it finds a 1935 example in the works of J.T. Farrell, author of the hard-boiled Studs Lonegan stories, set in Chicago. Both somewhat remote from the West Country streets where I hear it today.

Still, the *OED*'s etymology is compelling. It suggests that 'eggy' comes from the verb 'to egg', meaning 'to encourage' or 'to incite'. In the modern vernacular, then, 'to egg' is to 'wind up', while 'eggy' is to be 'wound-up'.

And the verb 'to egg' itself is even more interesting. It comes from the Old Norse *eggja* meaning a cutting 'edge' or sword: 'eggy' and 'edgy' are much the same thing. Another possibility, though less appealing, is that 'eggy' is simply a shortened form of 'aggressive' or 'agitated'. It doesn't exactly sound like either, but that doesn't rule out the possibility.

Sadly, hard evidence is lacking. You may trawl the word-banks of the world for 'eggy', but in vain. The *Guardian* once described a sitcom character as an 'eggy youth', but left that tantalizingly unexplained. Of course, this was the *Guardian*. It was probably supposed to say 'edgy'.

Enormity

Once on the BBC news, I watched a windswept reporter talking about an 'enormity' that had happened on the golf course at Carnoustie in Scotland. What could have happened? Had someone spit-roasted a caddie?

Not quite. What was being reported was that Paul Lawrie, a local man of modest aspirations, had just won the British Open. Extraordinary, then, but no 'enormity' was involved. The reporter meant 'scale' or 'magnitude', but he obviously thought that 'enormity' sounded more powerful.

Which it does, but only because there has, for the past 150 years, been general agreement that 'enormity' means something different to simple 'enormousness'. An 'enormity' is something abnormal or out of the ordinary, but in a very bad way.

'Extreme or monstrous wickedness,' says the *OED*, tracing the word back to the fifteenth century. 'A gross and monstrous offence.' Not quite what you'd expect on the links at Carnoustie, unless you were enjoying a round with Hannibal Lecter.

But why should that be the case, when enormous simply means large? Well, that's what it means now. But enormous began by meaning 'monstrous or shocking', before that fell out of use, leaving us with the modern sense simply of unusual size.

Both words have their origin in the French *énorme*. For a while, from the fifteenth century onwards, there was an English adjective 'enorm', which meant at various times unusual, wicked and vast. According to Caxton, for instance, the crimes of Sodom and Gomorrah were 'enorm'.

All these words come ultimately from the Latin *enormis*. That simply means 'not *normis*', and *normis* turns out to have a simple concrete meaning. It was a carpenter's set square. So anything *enormis*, *énorme* or 'enorm' was crooked, bent, twisted, off-centre or freakishly large.

All of which makes 'enormity' a word for golf correspondents to avoid, except when someone actually has spit-roasted a caddy.

Fashionista

Fashionistas

From a review of a television fashion programme: 'Thenceforth the entire show turned into a kind of unofficial advert for Top Shop – or "To' Sho'" as nervous fashionistas allegedly call it.'

Who are these people? What are they nervous about? And how does mispronouncing monosyllables help?

We can at least answer the first question. 'Fashionistas' are people with an interest, professional or amateur, in modish clothes. Dedicated Followers of Fashion, to quote Ray Davies.

Like The Kinks' song, the word 'fashionistas' contains an element of mockery. For some reason, normal people doubt the seriousness of anyone with a consuming interest in handbags.

The Spanish -*ista* suffix, the equivalent of our 'ist', suggests political struggle. Remember the Sandinistas? While overthrowing the dictator Somoza and his American imperialist allies, this glamorous leftist group found time to spawn a range of attractive tee-shirts and posters.

They also inspired an album by The Clash. Humorous variants on the -*ista* theme duly appeared, for instance, Liverpool's Hattonistas. Their Che Guevara now hosts a radio chat show.

In 1993, a man called Stephen Fried coined the word 'fashionista' in a book called *Thing of Beauty: The Tragedy of Supermodel Gia*, using the political suffix with irony. Within a year, the term had appeared in the American newspapers and the irony had drained away.

By 1995, the *Evening Standard*'s New York diarist was commenting that the Fashion Mafia had taken to calling *themselves* 'the Fashionistas', either facing down the mockery or not noticing it.

'Fashion' itself comes from the Latin verb *facere*, 'to make'. From the early fourteenth century, it meant the way something was made, or a way of behaving. By Tudor times, people were talking of 'fashion' as the prevailing style of a time. Far from being a modern affliction, the aesthetic dictatorship known as 'the fashion' has been with us since the late sixteenth century.

The one thing that does not go out of fashion is fashion itself.

Feedback

'And now some feedback,' says the announcer, only to be drowned by a terrifying electronic screech.

It could happen. Today 'feedback' is jargon, meaning 'response', 'reaction' or 'listeners' letters', but it has other meanings.

In the early days of electricity, engineers talked about 'feeding' equipment with current, electricity being the equipment's nourishment. To 'feed' is Old English, first recorded in the tenth century.

In the 1920s, the first 'feedback' radio circuits took some of their output and wired it back into the input. 'Positive feedback', like flattery, boosts output but promotes instability. 'Negative feedback', on the other hand, cuts output but improves stability.

The idea that processes could be controlled by monitoring their outcomes and adjusting input accordingly proved to have widespread application. 'Feedback' was borrowed by mechanical engineering, biochemistry, medicine, ergonomics, engineering, anthropology, education and many forms of psychology.

None of which explains its triumph in everyday speech. Every occasion and official publication now includes an appeal for 'feedback'. Some insist the idiom emerged in the 1950s, but evidence is scarce.

In 1969, it was still technical. President Nixon wanted people video-recorded as they watched one of his speeches. The engineers and psychologists handling the assignment called it 'feedback'. By 1971, however, the hippies had adopted it, talking about getting 'good feedback' about a concert or a meeting. The gulf between technology and the street had been crossed, but how?

It might have been scientific education, but it could also have been young men with guitars. Acoustic 'feedback', also known as 'howlround', was a nightmare for engineers, but after October 1965, when the Beatles used it on 'I Feel Fine', pop musicians adored it. The sound from your amplifier rattles the strings of your guitar: before you know it, you're playing 'Star Spangled Banner'.

Celebrity endorsement, loud noise: 'feedback' never looked back.

Now please don't forget to complete your response form when you finish reading.

Feisty

People are 'feisty'. But you also get sentences like this, in the business pages: 'the most cantankerous and feisty analyst meeting I have ever been to'.

The confusion is widespread. My local paper reviewed a Susan Sarandon film and headlined it 'Susan shines as a feisty mother'. The review beneath the headline went on to tell us that she was a 'flighty mum', which is not the same thing at all. But Susan Sarandon is always called 'feisty'. Some actresses are.

No one would dream of applying the word to the likes of Gwyneth Paltrow, who floats around being beautiful. But it clings like mud to, say, Holly Hunter, for whom 'Don't call me "feisty"!' has become almost a mantra.

It is an adjective applied to aggressive sports personalities, battling businessmen and people who have their work cut out. It especially suits those actresses who play memorable characters, struggling against such obstacles as unremarkable looks and diminutive stature.

It seems to come from 'fist', a little-known noun that rhymes with 'iced'. Preserved in the dialect of the American South, it means a small dog.

Before Ms Sarandon and Ms Hunter consult their lawyers, it should be pointed out that the aspect of the dog referred to is its aggression: 'feisty' means argumentative, touchy, excitable. Applied to women, 'feisty' implies, at the very least, flirtatiousness.

Interestingly, the word 'fist' – with the same pronunciation – originally meant a foul smell, particularly from breaking wind or 'fisting'. The *Dictionary of American Slang* suggests, rather fancifully, that the dog – in Elizabethan English, a 'fisting cur' or 'fisting hound' – acquired its name because you could blame it if you had the misfortune to break wind in company.

This explains the nineteenth-century American schoolboy insult 'feisty-breeches'. Enough to make anyone aggressive.

It all tends to explain why Ms Hunter – born in Georgia – so dislikes 'feisty'. It also makes you glad to have missed that analyst meeting.

Finesse

Now that ripping up graveyards and concreting over children's playgrounds is discouraged, property developers are becoming experts in the art of public relations.

'We will work with the local community,' one consortium recently told a public meeting, 'to finesse existing planning permissions.'

As a member of the audience, waiting to hear about the 500 houses and a supermarket this particular group planned to build alongside an area of outstanding natural beauty, I was baffled. What did they mean? And would it be legal?

No doubt the spokesman intended to say that the plans they had already agreed with the local council would be 'polished' or 'refined' with the help of local people. But that fashionable bit of business jargon led him astray.

Turning up first as a noun, in the sixteenth century, 'finesse' was indistinguishable from 'fineness'. Both meant excellence or delicacy of work. Later, 'finesse', effectively no more than a Francophile pronunciation of the same word, encompassed the same qualities in human behaviour.

But by the time the verb arrived, the reputation of the French had changed, and 'finesse' had come to mean 'cunning' or an 'artful strategy'. 'To finesse' made its debut as a technical term in the game of whist, the rules of which were formulated in the 1740s.

To 'finesse' a trick in whist (and later in bridge) is to win while holding back your highest card: it's a way of getting what you want without revealing your strength. When Jane Austen wrote in 1814 that an associate had been 'finessed into an affection', she meant he had been manoeuvred into it without feeling a thing.

To 'finesse' a deal is to appear to give something small in order to gain a lot. 'To use artifice,' according to one modern dictionary, 'to trick', according to another.

Our property developers may well be playing their cards straight. But their language suggests they have a few hidden in their socks.

Firm

From a *Daily Telegraph* television preview: 'Tina's father Don is the "godfather" on the block, organizing his "firm", and nobody messes with him . . .' No doubt Her Majesty the Queen takes a similar line. 'Firm' is used affectionately, even proudly, by members of organizations ranging from criminal gangs to the House of Windsor. Why?

You might think a 'firm' is called that because it is 'solid'. But even a cursory reading of the City pages would disabuse you of that notion. There is a connection, but it is more remote.

A 'firm' in our sense originally meant a signature, still called a *firma* in Spanish, Portuguese and Italian. The word was adopted by English in the sixteenth century after we'd begun dealing with exotic foreigners.

We already had the adjective 'firm', meaning 'resolute' or 'fixed'. It was a fourteenth-century adaptation of the French *ferme*, a word that originally meant a commitment to rent a patch of agricultural land. Only later did it come to mean the business you carried out there.

Firma, 'firm', *ferme* and 'farm' all came from the Latin *firmus*, meaning 'settled'. To make a 'firm' agreement, you would use your 'firm' or signature.

The Italian *firma* also implies 'good name' or 'reputation'. That led eighteenth-century English writers to speak of businesses 'conducted under the firm of Smith and Jones'. By the nineteenth century it came to mean not just the business's name, but its very being.

At the same time, wits used it sarcastically of other organizations, some devoted to activities incompatible with membership of the Chamber of Commerce.

Thus, in the twentieth century, surgeons and physicians began to call themselves 'firms'. The wartime secret service, the Special Operations Executive, was known to some members as 'the Firm'.

So was the Kray brothers' gang, according to *Inside the Firm*, the autobiography of one member. Oh yes, it was also a common and affectionate word for a CID squad. Versatile indeed.

Footfall

Footfall

Imagine a word, coined by Shakespeare, used by Sir Walter Scott, taken as a title by Samuel Beckett, and now used only by retail executives and City analysts. Sad, isn't it? One minute 'footfall' was poetry, the next it was jargon.

'There's no question it's getting tougher,' moaned a man from a tea merchants, presenting his annual results. 'People are spending less freely and there's a lower footfall through our stores.'

He meant fewer people were going into his shops; but you don't get to be managing director using language like that.

All of which is some way from 'footfall's origins. It is recorded first in Shakespeare. He probably made it up, by analogy with 'nightfall' and 'rainfall'. He puts it in the mouth of Caliban, in *The Tempest*, when he complains that he is tormented by Prospero's spirits, which are like 'hedgehogs which / Lie tumbling in my barefoot way and mount / Their pricks at my footfall'. Nasty.

Thereafter, it lived on as a poetic alternative to 'footstep', used particularly when the writer's attention is taken by the sound of pattering feet. Here's a typical example from *A Princess of Thule*, a forgotten bestseller of 1873 by William Black: 'He did not hear her approach, her footfall was so light.'

The word also found a place in nature writing, especially in the context of horses, whose gait seems to suit 'footfalls' rather than the more deliberate 'footsteps'. None of this explains the recent vogue for 'footfall' among those whose careers are dedicated to building a Britain fit for shoppers, and almost no one else.

Perhaps there is some connection with Samuel Beckett's 1975 *Footfalls*, a typically appealing play about a woman walking up and down muttering. She wouldn't want to try that in the High Street. Some kinds of footfall are less welcome than others.

Freak

Contrasting uses of the word 'freak': on the one hand, our 'control freak' Government; on the other, a new television programme, for and about disabled people, provocatively entitled *Freak Out*.

To call your show *Freak Out* is to 'reclaim' a word that has been used to insult you. Just as some homosexuals now proclaim themselves 'queer', and psychiatric patients bandy around the word 'mad', these disabled people have adopted 'freak'. Naturally the word has only been reclaimed for those inside the group to use.

Interestingly, 'freak' is not inherently unkind. Appearing in late Tudor times, possibly from an Old English word meaning 'to dance', it meant a whim or a sudden change of mind. It had no connection with deformity or deficiency until the nineteenth century, when it turned up in an American euphemism, 'freak of nature', meaning a farm animal that could be exhibited in a fairground. Hence, years later, the horrible playground gibe recycled in Channel Four's programme title.

Still in the States, 'freak' soon came to mean an enthusiast. The first citation was in 1908 ('One of your kodak freaks'). In 1946, Duke Ellington admitted to being 'a train freak', good news for the image of 'gricers' everywhere.

The hippies of the 1960s introduced us to 'speed freaks' and 'acid freaks', and enthusiasm shaded into addiction. 'Control freaks' are addicted to order and not only over their own lives. It has replaced older, pseudo-Freudian insults like 'anal-retentive'.

The first 'control freaks' are said to have appeared in Michael Herr's 1977 novel *Dispatches*, based on his experiences as a reporter in Vietnam. It was borrowed for the first Vietnam movies, *The Deerhunter* and *Apocalypse Now*, and later became almost a badge of honour for film actors and directors.

Michael Herr used the term to mean those who 'always . . . had to know what was coming next'. A reasonable description of the mindset in Downing Street, perhaps, but not a realistic aspiration for any mere mortal.

Funky

Desk accessories in novelty plastic; the floppy hairdo associated with Gwyneth Paltrow; an 'inappropriate' outfit worn by a woman thrown out of Harrods. All 'funky', at least according to the *Daily Telegraph*, the oracle on such matters.

'Funky' today is just a term of approval, but sometimes it has other implications. For instance, white people who say they live in a 'funky' area are implying that it is racially mixed. Because 'funk' is a black thing.

Not to D.H. Lawrence, however. He saw 'funk', meaning fear or cowardice, in all directions, except perhaps in the mirror. His 'funk' was mid-eighteenth-century slang, from Oxford and the public schools. There was a verb, 'to funk', meaning to flinch from something, and even a 'funky', amusing when you stumble upon it in Victorian literature. 'I do feel somewhat funky,' says a character in one novel of 1845. Well, I laughed.

In the fourteenth century, however, there was a 'funk', possibly Dutch in origin, that meant a 'spark'. Later it meant the mossy stuff on trees, used to kindle a pipe. It stank. And when 'funk' resurfaced in seventeenth-century Virginia, it meant a smell, particularly that of tobacco smoke. In American dialects it has meant a stink ever since.

The modern 'funky' is recorded first in the early 1950s, in the context of jazz and blues, meaning 'authentic' or 'earthy'. Later it was used to suggest something was 'authentically black'. In the 1970s, it became the label for a style, shoehorned into the names of songs as inauthentic as 'The Funky Gibbon'.

There is a connection between 'funk', meaning smell, and 'funky', meaning earthy and raunchy, but you won't be reading it here. The curious should seek out Jonathon Green's excellent *Cassell Dictionary of Slang*. It explains, for instance, why 1970s soul diva Millie Jackson sang that she liked being a mistress because it meant washing 'nobody's funky drawers but your own'.

Gatekeeper

The world is suddenly full of 'gatekeepers': Rupert Murdoch, for instance, and Bill Gates; the people behind the desk at the social security office and your local GP; and the panoply of press assistants surrounding Tony Blair.

The word was coined in the sixteenth century to mean one who guards an entrance. A 'gate', recorded as early as the eighth century, was the hole in the wall before it was the wrought-iron arrangement some of us have at the end of our garden paths.

The new uses are figurative, rather than literal. A 'gatekeeper' has no real gate, but nonetheless controls access to someone important, a party leader, for instance. In the new hierarchy of political life, this is a powerful position: the 'gatekeeper' comes second only to the 'spin doctor'.

The local GP, meanwhile, is a 'gatekeeper' because it has become his or her job to guard the NHS's riches from the discontented peasantry, assisted only by a receptionist modelled on Cerberus. The same for DSS clerks, only more so.

But the vogue for 'gatekeeper' seems to stem from the world of computers, whose jargon is often tinged with the bogus medievalism of the 'sword and sorcery' games beloved of the early hackers. A 'gateway' is an 'interface' or connection between two computers. Someone or something that tries to control that is a 'gatekeeper'.

Step forward Mr Rupert Murdoch, with your digital 'set-top box' through which so much television is increasingly squeezed. Step forward Mr Bill Gates, with your constant efforts to insert yourself electronically into all (well, most) human transactions.

The 'gatekeeper' of old kept people out or he let them in. Unlike these characters, he didn't normally extract a levy from them as they passed. That was normally the preserve of different specialists: the 'tollkeeper' and the 'highwayman'.

Gay

You don't have to look far to find the word 'gay' in the newspapers. But how often do you see it used to mean 'happy, cheerful, light-hearted'?

But recently I stumbled on that traditional meaning in a paragraph about a stately home in Hull: 'The aristocratic architect used to grow guavas, paw-paws and pineapples there, and give them to local gentry. Such gay social proceedings . . .'

Is this the start of a counter-revolution? As it happens, the now-standard 'gay', meaning homosexual, is out of fashion with many of those who favoured it. Having become the norm, it has little value either as a piece of insider code or a provocation. For the latter, the older 'queer' has been successfully revived.

There are few laughs in etymology, but the *OED* might raise the hint of a smile with its suggestion that 'gay' comes from an Old High German word, *wahi*, meaning 'pretty'. Who knows. By the time we borrowed it from the French, in the fourteenth century, it already meant joyful, cheerful, merry and brightly coloured.

It was from the seventeenth century that things began to go adrift. 'Gay' came to imply wantonness or dissipation. A 'gay man' was a womanizer. A 'gay' woman, to the Victorians, was a prostitute.

But what of our modern 'gay'? The source is the slang of American tramps and hobos. From the turn of the twentieth century, the word 'gay-cat' described young, inexperienced and half-hearted tramps. Undoubtedly some of these formed certain attachments, and by the 1930s the word always implied that. During World War II, homosexual men began to call themselves 'gay'.

In Britain it was certainly known, as a piece of colourful underworld slang, by the 1960s. But it only entered the mainstream around the English-speaking world in 1969, when the Gay Liberation Front made its debut.

But now things may be moving on again. Good news, especially, for anyone born on the Sabbath Day.

Geezer

Geezer

On the day examiners condemned 'slipshod, slangy expressions' in English A-level papers, the official spokesman of the Department of Culture declared that it did not want the Royal Parks 'ruined by a dodgy geezer selling a burger on a dirty old trolley'. No wonder kids are confused.

The word 'geezer' is certainly slang, but is it slipshod? It is vivid and colloquial, but you could not call it precise.

For a start, how old is a 'geezer'? In Britain, 'geezers' are just 'blokes', and they don't have to be old. There are also 'dodgy geezers' and 'diamond geezers'.

Across the Atlantic, however, 'geezer' is synonymous with age. They tell one another 'geezer jokes', complain about 'geezer-bashing' and even join geezer.com, an Internet site where 'older people' sell their handmade wares. As the site insists, 'today's geezer is a bright, experienced, talented person'. So it can't be him selling those greaseburgers in St James's Park.

When it appeared, in late Victorian times, it meant any old person, male or female. But soon it came to mean a disreputable male. Graham Greene used it in *Brighton Rock*, and 'geezers' featured extensively in the Ealing version of cockney.

The *OED* calls it a Northumberland pronunciation of 'guiser', defined as 'a masquerader or mummer'. The slang lexicographer Eric Partridge, meanwhile, suggested that it was borrowed from the Basque *giza*, a man, during the 1801–14 Peninsular War. If so, it stands alongside 'anchovy' in the rich catalogue of Basque-derived words in English.

Perhaps it reflects that other 'geezer', hanging on the kitchen wall in dodgy bedsits? Despite the efforts of the manufacturers, the domestic 'geyser' has been pronounced 'geezer' since its introduction in 1878, only seven years before the first recorded appearance of its disreputable homophone. There must be a connection.

Worn out, wheezing, found in disreputable surroundings and inclined to blow up unless given regular attention: and the water heaters are nearly as bad.

Gender

'Gender' is everywhere these days: 'gender differences', 'gender-based difficulties', 'gender issues'. It's amazing how many people are afraid of sex.

Because sex is the traditional word to use in discussing the difference between men and women. But increasingly sex means sexual intercourse and not much else.

Years ago, handed a form with the word 'gender' where I expected 'sex', I asked why. 'Because "sex" is offensive,' came the reply. There are some people, apparently, to whom those three letters are inherently shocking. So 'gender' it was.

'Gender' means 'kind', or 'sort', from the Old French *genre*. It is fourteenth century, and then it was indeed possible to say there were two 'genders' of people, male and female. So you could say 'You of the female gender, stand over there and wait 600 years for equality' but you couldn't discuss 'gender' as an idea.

It was really used in grammar. Scholars knew that there were, in most European languages, three 'kinds' or 'genders' of noun, each with its own behaviour. They called them male, female and neuter, although their relationship with the sex of the things they represent is not straightforward. In German, for instance, 'girl' is neuter. When you leave Europe, it gets worse. Tivunjo of Tanzania has sixteen genders.

The modern 'gender' is an invention of our own era. The *OED* attributes it to Alex Comfort, in 1963, before he discovered *The Joy of Sex*. Comfort and others, especially the feminists, used 'gender' to mean the sexual roles we acquire, leaving 'sex' to mean our innate sexual identity.

This was a reasonable idea, and worked well until the 1980s, when 'gender' became an academic and political buzzword. Soon Comfort's subtle distinction was lost and bureaucrats were handing round forms with 'gender m/f' on them.

'Gender' is ambiguous, politically loaded, and confusing to those learning English. Still, it doesn't offend anyone – and that's what counts.

Glitz

You will recall the scene in *The Merchant of Venice* when the Prince of Morocco is invited to guess which of three caskets contains a portrait of Portia, thereby winning her hand.

He opens the attractive gold box, but instead of the picture finds a skull with a sarcastic rhyme rolled up in its eye socket. 'All that glisters is not gold,' it begins. Shakespeare would have been a boon to the game-show industry.

The proverb predates the play, so we have long been wary of things that glister, and things that glitter (that being merely a modern variant). But what are we to think about 'glitz'? Is 'glitz' good, worthwhile and admirable; or is it dishonest, tawdry and distasteful?

For instance, when the fashion designer Gianni Versace was shot dead in Miami, colleagues queued up to offer moving tributes. Here's Bruce Oldfield's comment: 'He was a master at what he did . . . He was uncompromisingly glitzy. He was glitz, glitz, glitz.'

On the other hand, when music critic Geoffrey Norris wanted to attack pianist Arcadt Volodos, prematurely hailed as the new Horowitz, he said his playing was 'glitzy'. Context is everything, it seems.

In origin, 'glitz' seems to have been a bad thing. 'Glitzy' came first, in the mid-1960s, apparently from the German *glitzern*, meaning to glitter, possibly via Yiddish. It is first recorded in the *New York Times*, in reference to advertising, and it was soon widely used in the media, fashion and the arts.

Nonetheless, 'glitzy' was usually used negatively, often coupled with words like tacky, cheap and vulgar. 'Glitz' came later, a 'back-formation' from 'glitzy'. And again, the early definitions are damning: flashiness, ostentation, superficial display.

But that was in the 1970s, when such things were still frowned upon. In the 1980s, ostentation and vulgarity, if expensively acquired, became the height of style. And 'glitz' lost its pejorative note. Things are slightly different, of course, if you are a concert pianist.

Grandstanding

Grandstanding

When a cabinet minister suggested locking away disturbed people with no record but 'a tendency' to commit crimes, he was accused of 'grandstanding'.

Sadly, this charge might have disturbed him more if people had understood what it meant.

A 'grandstand' is the principal seating area in a sports arena. To 'grandstand' is to perform with the aim of winning applause rather than the match.

Originally each racetrack had a 'Grand Stand' modelled on the one at Ascot built in 1838. 'Grand' is self-explanatory: it suggests something splendid, rather than a few planks on the side of a hill.

But 'stand' is a multifaceted word dating back to the Dark Ages. It has thirty-odd different meanings, of which one, first heard in the seventeenth century, is 'somewhere you stand to watch horse-racing'. It derives from the medieval idea of the 'stand' as the station of a soldier or a hunter.

Although there were lots of 'Grand Stands' at individual sports grounds, we generally spoke of 'stands'. But in America all 'stands' were grand, and it was there that the idea of 'grandstand play' developed.

While we concentrated on sportsmanship and the art of graceful defeat, the Americans stormed ahead with techniques designed to enhance the show-business aspects of professional sport.

'Grandstand play' or simple 'grandstanding' was in regular use by the end of the nineteenth century, in the context of such tricks as rolling around the field or diving headlong to make an 'impossible' catch in baseball.

By the first years of the twentieth century it had even been used in reference to politics, with Teddy Roosevelt a noted exponent of the art. Interestingly, though, contemporary accounts insist that Roosevelt's attempts at 'grandstanding' generally favoured his opponents.

There may be a lesson here for some home-grown politicians of more recent vintage.

Grass

Never before have Britons been so willing to inform on their friends and neighbours through the information lines and television programmes provided by the authorities. And yet, to be accused of 'grassing' is a terrible thing.

'Grass' started as a noun, meaning a police informant, and was first heard in low-life slang in the early 1930s. The *Guardian* once proposed that this 'grass' was short for 'grass snake'. It makes a sort of sense, snakes being a byword for perfidiousness since the days of Aesop's fables, not to mention the Book of Genesis. But although this explanation seems plausible, there is a better one.

'Grass' seems to have come from the word 'grasshopper', which preceded it in approximately the same role. It is rhyming slang, which was invented by nineteenth-century criminals before being taken up more widely.

Some dictionaries insist that the rhyme in this case is between 'grasshopper' and 'shopper'. A 'shopper' here is not someone who buys things but a person who 'shops' you to the authorities. That verb, by the way, is nothing new. As far back as the Tudors, the verb 'to shop' meant either to lock someone else up or betray them to those who would.

On the other hand, in Edwardian times, 'grasshopper' was recognized rhyming slang for 'copper'. In other words, a 'grass' meant a policeman before it meant the policeman's informant. This seems the most convincing explanation, and is certainly the best documented.

The verb 'to grass' had existed in nineteenth-century slang, meaning 'to knock someone over' (on to the grass) or even to kill them. But under pressure from the new noun, it took on its present meaning.

Still underworld slang in the days of *Z Cars*, it is now common in offices and factories and playgrounds. True acceptance will only come, however, when *Crimewatch* is renamed *Grassing Time*, and that is not likely just yet.

Grok

Feast your eyes on this headline, from *Slashdot*, an online magazine for computer programmers: 'What the Linux community needs to grok'.

The 'Linux community' is not an obscure monastic order, although it might as well be. It means people who understand Linux, a frightening computer operating system that has the virtue of not being made by Microsoft. And 'grok'? Luckily, the author glosses it for those whose Geek is rusty. He means something the Linux community must 'understand deeply' or 'get clearly into its collective head'.

And what must it 'grok'? That Linux lovers must compromise with the real world, perhaps even adopting its vocabulary. On the other hand, we may yet end up adopting theirs.

'Grok' came into English in the early 1960s, from the Martian – and there's a phrase you don't often read. In 1961, the science-fiction writer Robert Heinlein wrote a novel called *Stranger in a Strange Land*. 'Martian' words spice up the story. To 'grok', readers learned, had a literal meaning: 'to drink'. But metaphorically it meant 'to commune with' or 'to understand by intuition'.

Here's the novel's explanation: ' "Grok" means to understand so thoroughly that the observer becomes a part of the observed – to merge, blend, intermarry, lose identity in group experience. It means almost everything that we mean by religion, philosophy, and science – and it means as little to us [because we are from Earth] as color means to a blind man.'

Deep . . . The Californians were the first Earthlings (all right, near-Earthlings) to adopt the word. By the mid-1960s, it was part of the vocabulary of the smart set chronicled in *Esquire* and *Playboy*. And then, mysteriously, it entered the jargon of the hardcore computer fraternity and stayed there.

In today's computer world, to 'grok' a program or a language is simply to have a 'good enough' understanding of it. But that's an achievement in itself, as anyone who uses a computer will 'grok' already.

Hacker

Shock news: whoever keeps causing all these computer viruses, it's not likely to be a hacker.

'Hackers' are usually defined as people who gain access to other people's computers to find information or do damage. But viruses are *programs* that gain access to other people's computers, find information and do damage. The people who make viruses are virus writers. In other words, programmers. A subtle distinction — especially when your hard disk has just been erased.

Interestingly, older computer experts never use 'hacker' in a negative way. To them, a person doing damage is a 'cracker', a 'cyberpunk' or a 'phreak'. A 'hacker' is someone who really knows computers, making them do fast, useful and ingenious things.

For most people, however, 'hacking' and 'hackers' have destructive associations. This is perhaps because 'to hack' means 'to chop off'. Emerging out of Old English in around 1200, it was often used in the context of the human head.

Before computers, an English person asked to name a 'hacker' might have suggested a footballer notorious for his harsh tackling. To 'hack' was to bring down illegally, in both soccer and rugby.

The Americans have a different nuance. Since the early part of this century they have used 'to hack' or 'to hack it' to mean 'to solve a problem'. A metaphor, perhaps from 'hacking' through undergrowth, this was the source of the positive idea of the computer 'hacker', recorded first in 1976.

A year later, a man called Gates founded a little company called Microsoft, and soon the exciting hobby had become boring and corporate. Enthusiasts who failed to become billionaires soon found there was fun to be had in illicitly tampering with other people's machines.

Unsympathetic observers, failing to observe the distinction between the two groups, misapplied the innocent old term to the new crime, which emerged in the 1980s. A mistake, then: but with 800 years of destruction behind it, 'hacking' didn't really deserve much more.

Handbag

'It was handbags out there for a while,' says the football manager, describing a near-riot among his highly disciplined professionals. 'But nothing serious.'

In sport, 'handbags' means an off-the-ball incident that stops just before anyone is hospitalized. It refers obliquely to such phrases as 'handbags at dawn' or 'handbags at ten paces'.

The image is of a spat between middle-aged women or camp homosexuals, the 'handbag'-toting targets of much 1960s and 1970s 'comedy'. Either way, the idea is to downplay the seriousness of the incident, impugn the masculinity of the combatants and discourage them from doing it again. Such is the psychology of sport.

Of course, the reference may be to that other 'handbag', the one associated with Mrs Thatcher, who had a tendency to 'handbag' those with whom she disagreed.

The source was an unnamed backbencher, who said in 1982 that 'she can't look at a British institution without hitting it with her handbag'. The accusation clung to her as tightly as she gripped the bag in question, which was eventually sold for £100,000 in a charity auction.

These days 'handbag' is a comical word. 'Handbag House', a dance music named after the practice of gyrating around the bag in question, never lived down its name. Then there's the human 'handbag', a man employed to accompany an otherwise unaccompanied woman to fashionable events.

But when Oscar Wilde gave the accessory a starring role in his 1899 comedy, *The Importance of Being Earnest*, was it inherently funny? It seems unlikely: for a start, Oscar's handbag is a decent-sized weekend bag, not a sliver of leather containing a lipstick, a nail file and a guide to calorie-counting. It had to be, for a baby to fit in it.

Nor was it a woman's thing, necessarily. George Bernard Shaw had just been out to get himself one, according to his letters. They do not reveal, however, whether he ever hit anyone with it.

Hassle

'Stop giving me this hassle,' shouts the exasperated mother in the supermarket as her little darlings ransack the sweet counter. Would her own mother have said that to her?

Possibly, depending on her age. But it wouldn't have been known to her grandmother, unless she was either an American entertainer or a Cumbrian farmer.

The 'hassle' we know is a row, a difficulty or a problem. The noun appeared first in print in America in 1945, in a story about a musician who had given up creating bands 'after booking hassels'. The spelling is peculiar, but the idiom is exactly that of the supermarket mum.

The modern version appeared slightly later. And then came the verb, by the end of the 1950s. To 'hassle' someone was to argue with them or cause them a nuisance. We picked it up at the time of the 'beats' and hippies and never lost it. Today it is widely used in most areas of society, along with such throwbacks as 'laid-back' and 'freak out'.

But we may only have taken back a word that was British in the first place. In William Wilkinson's 1878 *Dialect of Cumbria*, 'hassle' (also 'haggle') is defined as 'To hack at: to cut with a blunt knife, which requires a sawing motion.'

Is there a connection between sawing through rough terrain and dealing with the tiresome problems of life? Possibly, but it is hard to imagine why a decidedly agricultural Cumbrian word should turn up half a century later on the lips of American entertainers.

The Americans believe 'hassle' to be a blend, composed from equal parts of 'haggle' and 'tussle'. It happens: 'meld' is a blend of 'melt' and 'weld'; 'prissy' combines 'prim' and 'sissy'. But most such blends turn out to have been invented, usually by Lewis Carroll.

The language has no shortage of words for trouble and nuisance. Who would want the 'hassle' of inventing another one?

Heartsink

Doctors abuse their patients, you know: it's their way of getting their own back on us for demanding antibiotics when we have a cold. And they do it by calling us names.

Not as individuals, usually, but as types. There are the 'worried well', for instance, who have nothing wrong with them but think they might have. And then there are the 'heartsink patients', who are much more 'difficult', to use a perennial euphemism.

'Heartsink' patients are difficult in many different ways. They are, according to the literature of GP training, dependent, demanding, manipulative, self-destructive and much more. The worst thing about them, though, is that they get their doctors down: when 'heartsink' patients walk in, the GP's heart begins to sink.

The syndrome was first identified, and the label created, in a paper by a New England psychiatrist, Dr James Groves, writing in 1981. He called them 'HeartSinkers', which is less ambiguous, since what he was really writing about was the feelings of doctors.

As one who knows many doctors, I would be the last to suggest that this term implies that medical people are in any way self-centred. It is just a pity that they didn't use their labelling skills to say something about the people clogging their surgeries rather than their own feelings.

One of the reasons 'heartsink' has stuck, I suspect, apart from its solidly Germanic sound, is that it carries an echo of another word, used since the sixteenth century but now almost forgotten. The word is 'heart-sick', defined in the *OED* as 'depressed and despondent, esp. through "hope deferred" or continued trouble'.

Precisely the lot of many NHS users, is it not? Calling them 'heartsick patients' rather than 'heartsink patients' might not cure them, but it would serve as a reminder that they are not a problem: they're people with a problem.

Of course, I don't have to put up with them.

Heist

Heist

The citizens of Birmingham must have wondered whether they had woken up on a different continent the day their morning paper informed them of a daring 'art heist' in the city.

Newspaper subeditors need short words to describe complex misdemeanours. But how informative was 'heist' to readers not brought up on hard-boiled crime fiction? Wouldn't 'theft' have done just as well?

A 'heist', as lovers of the genre will know, is a robbery. For a century, 'heist' and the verb 'to heist' have applied to everything from hold-ups and even shoplifting back in the late 1920s, to elaborate burglaries today.

The word sounds as if it should have recent German roots, but it does not. In British criminal and police slang, to 'hoist' has long meant to shoplift. 'Heist' is a peculiar American pronunciation of that word, which has a long and disreputable history of its own.

'Hoister', defined as a shoplifter, was recorded in England as early as 1796; it was still in use in the 1970s. More specifically, however, 'to hoist' was an ingenious type of theft. You simply held someone upside down so coins fell from his pockets. By the nineteenth century, however, it meant to enter buildings illegally, either by 'hoisting' up windows or by 'hoisting' a colleague on your back to allow him to make an entry.

In all these cases, the word implies using a lifting action, and in everyday use 'to hoist' still means exactly that, even in America. It seems to have begun as a nautical term. 'Hoise! Hoise!' was the cry of fifteenth-century sailors, hauling up a sail with a block and tackle.

In time, this changed to the familiar 'hoist', meaning to raise into the air. When Hamlet talks of 'the engineer hoist with his own petard', he means a bomb-maker blown sky-high by his own bomb. Safer to stick to shoplifting or a little art theft, on the whole.

Holidays

Christmas is a changing festival. At one local shopping centre, the decorations have a circus theme. At the centre stands a group of mechanical clowns. Every eight minutes precisely the lead clown opens his mechanical mouth and roars 'Happy Holidays!', sounding not unlike Paul Robeson.

Then his companions sing a song. Not only is it free of religious references, it seems to have no specific cultural content whatsoever. True, it mentions 'Christmas', but only in the context of getting presents, a ritual now universal in British society, judging by the rich variety of those queueing in Woolworth's.

The American 'Happy Holidays!' is a seasonal greeting for all the modern world. It offends no one by being sufficiently vague to apply to everyone. It started as a way of encompassing both Christmas and Hanukkah, the Jewish festival that begins on 6 December.

Ambitious enough, but more recently it has expanded to encompass Kwanzaa, the traditional African-American winter festival invented by Dr Maulana Ron Karenga on 26 December 1966. Nor does it leave out those celebrating Ta Chiu, the Taoist festival of peace, which falls on 27 December. Adherents of Yule, the winter solstice, can acknowledge the greeting too.

The only group likely to be offended by 'Happy Holidays' are literal-minded atheists, since 'holiday' is a 1,000-year-old compound formed from 'holy' and 'day' and meaning a religious festival. It was only in the fourteenth century that it began also to mean 'a day without work'; before that, of course, the only days without work were religious festivals.

The modern idea of 'holidays', or a vacation, began in the fourteenth century too. The *OED*'s first reference to the 'Christmas holidays' comes in 1647, in Lord Clarendon's *History of the Rebellion in England*. A couple of years after that, of course, Christmas was banned by the Puritans.

Strangely, while we close down for a fortnight, the nation that invented 'Happy Holidays!' rarely finds the time to take any.

Honeytrap

A tabloid story secured when a man unknowingly confides in a female reporter is now known as a 'honeytrap', but for reasons that remain obscure.

One commentator described a newspaper's ensnaring of a sportsman thus: 'First it laid the honeytrap, then it set the bees on its victim.' In other words, the 'honeytrap' uses honey not to attract a victim, but to attract killer bees, which then attack. The kind of thing, in fact, that only ever happened in *The Man From U.N.C.L.E.*

Sadly, there is no such thing as a 'honeytrap', whether for luring sweet-toothed animals (step forward Winnie the Pooh), rallying apian assassins or simply trapping honey. A French proverb insists that 'more flies are caught by honey than by vinegar', but no trap is required. The honey in the newspapers' 'honeytraps' is similarly metaphorical.

The idea arose during the Cold War, when Westerners visiting the Soviet Union were sometimes blackmailed by Naughty Natasha or Lovely Lara whom they had just met in the hotel lobby. Peter '*Spycatcher*' Wright claimed that it had happened to Harold Wilson in Moscow. Others have suggested that we did similar things to Russians visiting London.

Why 'honeytrap'? Honey is sweet. And 'sweet', in English, has long been used of attractive and beloved people and things. 'Honey' or 'hinny' has been a term of endearment since the Middle Ages. Starting in Ireland and Scotland, it crossed the Atlantic before coming back via the movies.

The Americans also speak of 'a honey', meaning anything pleasing. In the 1960s, it was a surfer's girlfriend. In slang use, it describes all manner of unprintable activities. In a 'honeytrap', sex is the bait.

A 'sting', by the way, is another word for the same type of operation. It is 1930s criminal slang for a sudden and daring act of villainy. Apiarists can take heart: here, too, bees are innocent.

Horlicks

In the aftermath of the first London mayoral race, a nightmare for all sides, one leading Tory admitted that the party had 'made a bit of a Horlicks of it'. Well, at least they won't be losing any sleep.

This 'Horlicks', however, has nothing to do with Mr James Horlick's famous drink, created in 1883. It was described as 'a desiccated and granulated preparation of malt extract and milk as a food for infants and invalids'. No mention of troubled politicians, however.

Jonathon Green's *Cassell Dictionary of Slang* notes that 'horlicks' is a 1980s expression meaning 'a mess' and that its milieu is 'society'. Spot on, but it doesn't begin to explain why the upper classes should have come to associate a milk drink – rarely seen here, though still going well in India – with a mess.

Most likely, it is nothing to do with the meaning of the word and everything to do with its sound. It is a euphemistic substitution, akin to shouting 'Sugar!' when you drop something on your toe.

What word sounds a bit like 'Horlicks', has been known to mean 'a mess', and is not always welcome in polite society, despite being the standard anatomical term well into the eighteenth century? Here's a clue: it's plural, and it rhymes with 'Jackson Pollocks'.

Old English in origin (*beallucas*, since you ask), the anatomical term has had numerous figurative meanings. In James Joyce, for instance, it means a fool. In today's English, it means rubbish or nonsense.

But in the early twentieth century an Australian version spread everywhere. It used the word as a verb, meaning 'to make a mess', and as a noun meaning the mess itself. The phrase 'to make a Horlicks' sounds too similar for mere coincidence.

Of course, it's possible that what the man meant was that the Tories found the mayoral race just the thing they needed to calm, relax and reinvigorate them. So when is it going to start working?

Hub

After 'portals' were shown the door, Internet share pluggers scratched around for a new recommendation. They came up with the 'hub', which at least had the virtue of being a familiar word.

A 'hub' is the centre of a wheel. Originally an English dialect word, it was rare until it appeared in American dictionaries in the nineteenth century. The Americans even had an expression: 'up to the hub', meaning 'in deep'. Imagine a wagon train stuck in mud.

In our own era, 'hub' has become a key term in the computer world. In some types of network, it is the box from which cables extend, like the spokes in a wheel.

Internet entrepreneurs and their backers do not change wheels or install cabling. Their 'hubs' reflect a figurative sense, first heard in the nineteenth century when Boston was called the 'hub' of New England, the wheel around which everything revolved. Big airports, especially in the US, are often described in precisely this way.

The vogue for Internet 'hubs', particularly what are known as 'B2B hubs' or 'business-to-business hubs' reflects the realization that portals are not a licence to print money. When there were toll gates, people had to pay, because there was only one road. But people passing through a portal on their way to the Internet can always find an alternative a couple of mouse-clicks away.

The answer is supposed to be the 'hub', shamelessly talked up during the last quarter of 1999 by the same pundits who had previously boosted the portals.

Originally known as 'B2B market-makers', 'hubs' are Internet sites designed so that businesses trade among themselves without consumers holding prices down. They can buy ballpoints or offload surplus nuclear waste. The 'hub' takes a cut, or at least it tries.

'Hub' seems originally to have been the same word as 'hob', the hot part of a fireplace or stove. How apt. Those dealing in 'hub' shares must be careful not to get burnt.

Impact

When Glenda Jackson MP was campaigning to be Mayor of London, she complained repeatedly about the way the selection shambles was 'impacting on' voters.

Such a fine speaker of the English language might have done well to avoid an expression better suited to the plays what Ernie Wise wrote.

She could have said 'having an impact' or 'making an impact'. Instead she used what linguists call a 'conversion', turning a noun into a verb. No one minds 'to bicycle' or 'to download', because they arrived to describe new experiences. But 'to impact' is unnecessary and has unfortunate resonances.

'Impact' comes from the Latin *impactus*, meaning 'fixed'. In his *Natural History*, the Roman writer Pliny the Elder talked about 'humours' being *impactus* in the stomach. English translators, in the sixteenth century, simply adapted his adjective as 'impact' or 'impacted'.

'Impacted' has had medical associations ever since. It means things that are forced or squeezed together: teeth that can't find their way out of the jaw; bones so badly smashed that they are fused together. And much worse . . . The verb 'to impact', meaning to press or crush into a space, followed.

The noun 'impact', though, came from the science of mechanics, at the end of the eighteenth century. It referred to collisions between objects, and later between ideas, events and people. By the twentieth century, 'impact' was often a good thing.

Today the noun 'impact' usually relates to those figurative collisions and not the earlier crushings. But while ideas have 'impacted on' people and things for seventy years, it is still unusual. British dictionaries give the verb 'to impact' its literal, scientific and medical meanings.

'To impact on' appears only in US dictionaries, defined as 'have an impact on'. Such American language 'impacts on' us a little more every day. But if we are being crushed and squeezed, we don't seem to mind.

In Spades

A newspaper article about a sumptuous BBC costume drama dismissed fears about its cost. 'The taxpayer will get it back in spades,' it said. But wouldn't it be better to have it in money?

Despite the popularity of gardening, especially among television executives, this is not a reference to horticultural tools. 'In spades' comes from the vocabulary of card-playing, and is simply an 'intensifier', like 'very', 'extremely' or 'and how!'

The 'spades' in a pack of cards do indeed resemble a pointed spade, but the French, who invented them, call them *piques*, meaning 'pikes'. Our name rests ultimately on a mistranslation. 'Spades' is a sixteenth-century adaptation of the Italian *spade*, meaning not spades but swords. Swords had appeared on earlier Italian and Spanish playing cards, and on the tarot cards from which they derived.

'In spades' is an intensifier because spades are the highest-ranking suit in bridge, which, in its 'contract' form, was created in 1927. The *OED*'s first citation of the expression is in a 1929 magazine article by Damon Runyon, chronicler, if not inventor, of much Jazz Age slang. He describes certain Broadway characters as 'bums, in spades'.

John Major was famously criticized when he remarked that Hulme, a run-down area of Manchester, had 'problems in spades'. The suggestion was that the use of 'in spades' – innocent in itself – was unfortunate in the context of Britain's inner cities, where it might be thought to echo a racial epithet from the 1920s.

As it happens, the epithet in question – a reference to the colour of the playing card – was first used by black Americans about themselves, before being taken up by white enthusiasts for black culture.

The expression's hard-boiled film noir aura has kept it alive for years, but the unceasing vigilance of those who police the language for potential offence would suggest its days are numbered.

Inclusive

'Inclusive' is a handy word for any institution wishing to depict itself as modern, unsnobbish and forward-looking; for instance, the Conservative Party under the leadership of William Hague, the kind of comprehensive-educated, northern-accented individual who until recently would have been running the car park outside the party conference.

Modern Tories, though, are 'inclusive'. Having once detached themselves from most of the British population, they are now inclined to befriend everyone, including single mothers, gays, young people and those Asians who are not millionaires.

The word 'inclusive' neatly replaces other terms – 'cosmopolitan', 'multicultural', 'classless' – that are politically controversial. It is also popular in cultural circles, for similar reasons. Radio Three and the Proms and the Royal Opera must also become 'inclusive'. Its predecessors in this role, 'accessible', 'approachable' and 'user-friendly' are all associated with 'dumbing down' and the 'lowest common denominator'.

'Inclusive' means taking in, as opposed to leaving out, but it has not, until recently, been used of people. It is still so new in this sense that the newspapers have only just taken it out of inverted commas.

It only emerged in the late 1970s, when the first 'non-sexist' version of the Bible appeared in the US. Entitled *The Word for Us*, it was said to be 'restated in inclusive language'. Duly mocked and derided ('Our Mother . . .'), such 'inclusive' language has quietly become standard practice, at least for officialdom. Meanwhile educationalists practise 'inclusive' education, which means teaching disabled children alongside their unimpaired classmates. Both use 'inclusive' of people, which suggests they are the root of today's idiom.

Interestingly, 'inclusive' and its parent verb 'include' come from the Latin verb *includere*, which doesn't mean 'to bring in' but 'to shut in' or 'to confine'. One of the earliest appearances of the verb in English, in the fifteenth century, is in a story about someone who 'included' a wicked spirit by trapping it in a boiling pot. If only 'including' new Tory voters, and new listeners for Radio Three, was that easy.

Initiative

Authority loves 'initiative'. Not actual self-motivation, you understand, but the word.

When the Government opens a handful of dosshouses it's a 'Rough Sleepers Initiative'. When your council hands you a questionnaire about litter it's an 'Environmental Improvement Initiative'. And if your boss tells you not to be surly on the telephone, that's a 'Customer Care Initiative'.

In everyday parlance, however, 'initiative' isn't something you do, it's something you have. As *Chambers Dictionary* puts it, it is 'energy and resourcefulness enabling one to act without prompting from others'.

Both meanings, the official and the everyday, imply the start of some activity, because the word comes from the Latin *initium*, meaning 'entrance' or 'beginning'. Its first appearance in English is in William Godwin's *Enquiry Concerning Political Justice* of 1793.

Godwin borrowed the French *l'initiative*, and used it in a psychological sense, talking about the 'initiative' of actions, where we might say 'trigger' or 'stimulus'. But he also used it as a political term, to mean the power or right to propose legislation, and that version caught on.

By the middle of the nineteenth century it had found a more general application in such expressions as 'to take the initiative', now widely used in descriptions of ritualized conflict, for instance, sport and celebrity divorce. But it still has technical uses in political life. In Switzerland and several American states, an 'Initiative' is a device whereby citizens can call a referendum.

The 'initiatives' discussed every morning on the *Today* programme and in your company newspaper would seem to owe more to Ronald Reagan's 'Strategic Defense Initiative' of 1983, which popularized the term as a suitably vague replacement for such favourites as 'plan', 'scheme' and 'project'.

Because 'initiative' suggests that something is going to happen – but not what, or when – it continues to enjoy great popularity among those practising the art of leadership.

Item

Item

The tabloids occasionally refer to Prince Charles and Camilla Parker-Bowles as an 'item'. What a triumph for this little word, once a jokey bit of slang for American teenagers, now enjoying the limelight at the pinnacle of British society.

An 'item' is a couple. It allows newspapers to identify a relationship without specifying its precise nature. It merely says that two individuals have been seen together and accepted as one social unit rather than two. It solves the problem of how to refer to unmarried couples, especially those of advanced years.

Unfortunately, it's also a bit twee, being associated with teenage pop and gossip magazines which find it less middle-aged and respectable than 'couple' itself.

The word 'item' is actually a simple Latin adverb, meaning 'also'. In French, from the thirteenth century, and then in English from the fourteenth, it was used when composing a list, rather in the way that we might say 'next'. 'Item,' says Olivia in *Twelfth Night*, drawing up a list of her own attractions, 'two lips, indifferent red; item, two grey eyes, with lids to them; item, one neck, one chin, and so forth.'

Later, the word came to stand for the things on the list, particularly sums of money in a bill. The newspapers of the nineteenth century arranged their news as a list: the word 'item' now began to be used for the individual short pieces.

In the gossip and show-business columns pioneered by American newspapers, a sighting of an unexpected or secretive couple would make one of these 'items'. From making an 'item' it was a short step to *being* an 'item', at least in the trade jargon of journalists.

Eventually some anonymous show-business columnist let the expression find its way into print, and we have had it ever since. It seems to be here for a while. Twee or not, it has its uses.

Joined-up

Did you join up to the campaign for things to be 'joined-up'?

One of the first things that happened when Labour came to power after years of watching the Tories unravelling was to announce that it would be a 'joined-up government'.

The phrase was borrowed and modified by others. The then leader of the National Union of Teachers declared that he was in favour of 'joined-up thinking'.

Actually, he was in a good position to know what, if anything, that might mean. 'Joined-up' (from the Latin *jungere*, to join) refers to the kind of continuous handwriting that was taught in primary schools before teachers decided it would be better for everyone to use infant-school printing for the rest of their lives. Only recently has 'joined-up writing' been reinstated.

At my junior school we called it 'cursive', the expression 'joined-up' being considered babyish. But 'joined-up' is a descendant of 'join-hand' or 'joining-hand', terms used as long ago as the sixteenth century to characterize continuous handwriting.

The point about 'joined-up' writing is that it is grown-up: it is one of the milestones in life's journey, like wearing a watch or going to the corner shop without your mum.

Consequently, when the phrase first emerged, in the early 1990s, it meant 'mature' thinking, humour or debate. It did not involve joining anything together.

But then came the Internet, joining up computers all over the world so they could communicate at the speed of light. Heady stuff for governments weighed down by paperwork and procedures and forms to be completed in triplicate. In 'joined-up' they had a second-hand soundbite to describe this new world of efficiency, even if it had previously meant something different.

After much delay, a White Paper about 'joined-up government' appeared. It promised departmental co-ordination and revolutionary 'one-stop shops' in the High Street, where people could get forms to be completed in triplicate. And that was about the last time 'joined-up government' was mentioned.

Jollies

In a radio discussion of rape, a barrister remarked that violence was necessary to the rapist. 'That's how he gets his jollies,' he explained.

This cast rather a shadow over what I had always considered an entirely harmless word. Isn't a 'jolly' really a 'jollification', an outing, possibly involving singing, dancing and a ride in a charabanc? Not always, it seems.

'To get one's jollies' appears in the *OED*, with 'jollies' nervously glossed as 'a thrill of enjoyment or excitement'. But its 1957 citation, from the US humorist Max Shulman, indicates the kind of enjoyment that was meant: 'If she wasn't so goddam busy, then he wouldn't be thinking about getting his jollies elsewhere!'

Slang dictionaries are less reticent. To 'get one's jollies' is to enjoy oneself, certainly, but it is also to 'have sex'. A 'jolly' means many things, but one of them seems to be an orgasm. Clearly, some charabanc outings are more exciting than others.

It seems both uses have been with us for a very long time. 'Jolly' was adapted from the medieval French *jolif*, which meant lively, merry or amorous. Some suggest it is related to 'Yule', that being a traditional time of year for jollifications; others that it is from the Latin *gaudire*, to rejoice. No one really knows.

In Middle English, the adjective meant cheerful, happy and brave. By the end of the fourteenth century, it also meant lustful and wanton. In the nineteenth century, the noun came into being, meaning: a royal marine, a cheer, a person paid to praise or bid for an article as part of an auction ring, a bit of fun, an accomplice, a punch-up, a hoax, a type of small boat, and, in the plural, sexual favours.

The singular, in Britain at least, remains innocent. But to avoid confusion about 'jolly' you could revive 'jolly-up', a charming pre-1950s expression. Usually applied to a drinking session or informal dance, it has no known sexual connotations.

Jones

Reading a newspaper article, I stumbled on a reference to a man with 'a trash jones'. Perhaps it was a misprint. The man probably had 'trashed jeans'. Or was planning to 'thrash James'.

Luckily, I'd seen something similar a couple of days earlier, in a British novel about a group of single girls with 'a jones for chocolate'. Not much of a plot, but full marks for expanding the lexicon.

A 'jones' is a craving; indeed, a drug addiction. Some claim the term was common among jazz musicians as early as the 1940s. Heroin, rather than chocolate, was their poison and 'jones' is said to have referred to the drug as well as the addiction. Alternatively, there's a Jones Street in Greenwich Village where they are said to have lived.

Solidly black American, the expression later described less lethal cravings. From the mid-1980s, rapping artists talked about having 'a love jones'. The 'trash jones' – a liking for trashy things – was only a matter of time.

Interestingly, however, the word 'jones' has a long history in slang. Those of a nervous disposition should look away now.

'Jones' seems sometimes to have meant penis, as a variant on the familiar 'Johnson' or 'Mr Johnson': it is, after all, just the Welsh equivalent.

That 'Johnson' is sometimes linked with Jack Johnson, the legendary heavyweight. But it was actually recorded as early as 1863, in an account of a hellish journey across Canada: 'Neck frozen; face ditto . . . Johnson ditto'. I did suggest looking away . . .

But there are nineteenth-century references to a 'Mr Jones', a similar personification of the male member. It was a crowded field, however, what with those Johnsons, Jack Robinson, Johnny and, most notoriously, D.H. Lawrence's John Thomas of 1928.

But what of Mrs Jones? Sadly, she fared little better than her husband. In Edwardian times, to visit 'Mrs Jones' was to go to the lavatory. So much for keeping up with the Joneses.

Lady

'Lady' is back. And you didn't know it had gone away.

For thirty years the 'l-word' has been a crime against feminism, as has 'girl'. The only acceptable name for a female human is 'woman'.

But recently sports commentators have started referring once again to the 'ladies' powering round the track, regardless of the fact that they rarely stop to adjust their make-up. It's only a matter of time, though, judging by the compact-toting, handbag-wielding 'ladylike' fashions in the glossies.

Feminists think 'lady' is patronizing: flattery designed to oppress. Etymology suggests they may have a point.

Emerging in ninth-century England, the word looked something like this: *hlaefdiye*. Its male equivalent was *hlaford* or lord. Both words developed from *hlaef*, meaning a loaf. *Hlaford* was someone who 'keeps bread'. And *hlaefdiye*? That was someone who kneads it.

Throughout the Middle Ages, a 'lady' was the female head of a substantial household: the equivalent of the lord of the manor. But over time, 'lady' lost social rank, unlike lord. It became a courtesy title, like gentleman. But because it was once equivalent to 'lord', it retained social precedence, which is why we say 'ladies and gentlemen' rather than 'gentlemen and ladies'. And you thought it was chivalry.

For centuries it was a term of address: 'Thank you, lady.' Say that now and you become a character from *My Fair Lady*, or from Damon Runyon: after dwindling in cockney, it lived on in New York.

It has more intimate uses too. 'My lady wife', another favourite of the feminists, is recorded first in a Dickens letter of 1840. But Chaucer had imported the courtly love idea of the 'lady' as the object of a lover's devotion in the fourteenth century, and it has stayed with us. It can still be used to indicate any female consort, although the *OED* considers it vulgar.

Vulgar? A word favoured by ageing rock stars, nightclub owners and DJs? Impossible.

Lairy

When I heard a BBC trailer describing one of its female DJs as 'wanted for being mad and lairy in a built-up area', I thought I knew what the word meant. Now I'm not sure – and I doubt if the BBC knows either.

The reference books insist that 'lairy' is 'leery', a nineteenth-century adjective meaning 'knowing' or 'cunning'. The verb 'to leer' originally meant to look slyly, rather than lustfully. The reason for that, perhaps, is that 'leer', the Old English word *hleor*, once meant 'cheek'. To look slyly, you look across your cheek.

Later, 'leery' went off to America, where it meant 'nervous' or 'wary'. Our version became 'lairy', first seen in nineteenth-century accounts of underworld life. It means cunning, crafty or smug – excellent traits in a radio personality.

In the 150-odd years since then, 'lairy' has had various meanings around Britain, particularly in dialect and in the playground. In Suffolk, at the start of the twentieth century, it meant 'scatter-brained'; in Hull, in the 1920s, 'cheeky' or 'sarcastic'; in Leicestershire, in the 1950s, 'lucky' or 'jammy'; in Nottinghamshire, in the 1970s, 'mouthy' or 'stroppy'.

In London, in the 1930s, it was used for 'vulgar' or 'flashy', which is what it meant when it returned to fashion in the 1990s, in newspaper references to 'lairy waistcoats' and 'lairy suits'. This time round, though, the impetus seemed to be an influx of Australians, associated with Mr Murdoch's publications.

In modern Australian slang, a 'lair' is a layabout or hooligan; earlier, in the 1930s, it meant someone flashily dressed. And 'lair' came from 'lairy', first identified in Australia in the 1900s and meaning 'vulgar', just as it did in London.

So that's 'lairy': knowing, cunning, sly, crafty, smug, scatter-brained, cheeky, sarcastic, mouthy, vulgar, flashy and inclined to hooliganism. I wonder what slogan they would have used for someone they didn't like?

Lame

'And did you like what Father Christmas brought you, Jimmy?' 'No,' replies the brat. 'It was lame.'

Proof that buying a pony for Christmas is a bad idea. Except that Jimmy was given a Lego set, and doesn't even know that 'lame' relates to animals.

Among the young, 'lame' means feeble, unacceptable or hopeless. The expression is understood by any child who watches a lot of American television, which means all children. Even the 101 Dalmations now appear to live in Kansas.

Here we have 'lame excuses' – we get lots of practice – but generally 'lame' has stayed in the stableyard, where most of us never venture. But the horse and the range are central to the Americans' idea of themselves, and 'lame' has stayed relevant.

The word is at least 1,200 years old, Old English, and originally meant crippled or paralysed in some way. Only later did it apply specifically to the legs. By the fourteenth century, figurative uses had appeared. In *Troylus & Criseyde*, Chaucer says, and I translate, 'Don't blame me if my words are lame. I'm only telling you what it says here.' This disingenuous remark has done little to help generations of students.

Subsequently, abstract things – arguments, propositions, narratives, excuses – could sometimes be 'lame', perhaps because they 'proceed' or 'collapse'.

But while we lost interest when we no longer had horses to worry about, the Americans continued to use the word. It gradually evolved until it began to express disappointment and disgust, probably via the 1950s black word for a square or a social leper: 'a lame'.

'Lame duck', meanwhile, is an eighteenth-century City expression, meaning a person who couldn't pay his debts. From there, though, it moved on to mean a crippled ship. Now it is most commonly heard in the context of politics on both sides of the Atlantic, where crippled birds of the genus *Anas* have in living memory occupied both presidency and premiership.

Leverage

Leverage

'The bank has a strong brand and our plans are to leverage this in all of our communications,' said a man from a leading British bank, discussing his marketing strategy. Good idea, but wouldn't using the English language be more effective?

Here's another ugly noun-to-verb 'conversion'. But the real problem with 'to leverage' is that its meaning is obscure.

'To leverage' does mean something in the context of the business pages, especially in American newspapers. It means to speculate using borrowed money, expecting the profits of your speculation to outstrip the interest on your borrowings. A highly 'leveraged' company is one that has high borrowings and little money of its own.

The word appeared first in the 1930s, but its heyday was the 1980s, when 'leveraged buyouts' of underperforming companies were all the rage. One particularly grotesque example even provided the plot of a hit film: *Wall Street*. But our marketing man's 'leverage' has only the vaguest connection with that, unless his bank plans to start borrowing wildly with only its letterheads as security.

In physics and engineering, 'leverage' is force applied by the use of a 'lever', a thirteenth-century word for a metal or wooden bar used to prise open doors and lift heavy objects. Both words come from the French *lever*, to lift. 'Leverage' was big in the age of steam engines and canal boats, which is why it crept into Victorian speech as a figurative term meaning 'strength' or 'muscle'. People began to speak about having the 'leverage', social or political, to get what they wanted. From there it was a short step to business jargon.

So, when the man from the bank says he wants to 'leverage' its brand in all its communications, what he really seems to have meant is that he wanted to use the strength of its name. So why didn't he say that?

Lifestyle

One of the joys of being a magazine editor is being able to act on your prejudices. So no one was surprised when the editor of one fogeyish weekly announced that he'd banned 'lifestyle', despite the fact that his magazine was full of it.

The word, meaning features based around shopping and relationships, has its uses. It's journalistic jargon, perhaps unfairly associated with Harold Evans, editor of the *Sunday Times* in the 1960s.

You might recall the *Sunday Times* as the liberal newspaper that campaigned for the victims of Thalidomide. But others celebrate it for assembling recipes, ski-ing hints and the musings of Jilly Cooper into a mix that Evans labelled 'Look!' but others called 'lifestyle'.

'Lifestyle' meant catering for readers, particularly women, whose interests went beyond politics and plane crashes. It was both editorially lively and commercially rewarding, with a strong interest in the goods advertisers wanted to promote: French saucepans, scuba-diving gear, Danish furniture.

Business now adopted 'lifestyle' as a handy label for products selected to match a glamorous way of life. Habitat offered 'lifestyle' shopping. C & A, on the other hand, did not.

Earlier, in 1961, the *Guardian* noted: 'The mass-media continually tell their audience what life-styles are "modern" and "smart".' But then 'life-style' still had a hyphen, a remnant of its respectable origins in the world of psychology.

It was actually the invention of Alfred Adler, the third big name in psychoanalysis after Freud and Jung. He invented two terms that thrive: the other was 'inferiority complex'.

Writing in the 1920s, in German, Adler created a new compound noun: *Lebenstil*. It was subsequently translated as both 'lifestyle' and 'style of life', although today's Adlerians insist on the latter. This 'life-style' meant the dominant shape of a person's life, based on his or her own perception of reality, however warped.

'Lifestyle', meanwhile, is sometimes used today as a euphemism for wife-swapping. Saucepans and scuba-diving were probably a better bet.

Magic bullet

Politicians like the idea of the 'magic bullet', an instant solution for any problem from collapsing schools to Third World debt. But sadly, they only raise it to tell us there is no such thing.

Metaphors can be dangerous, and this one is worse than most. According to the invaluable *Facts on File Dictionary of Twentieth-Century Allusions*, the original 'magic bullet' was the first effective treatment for syphilis. Paul Ehrlich, the German doctor who developed it in the first years of the century, called it Salvarsan, which means salvation. 'Magic bullet' was its nickname.

Since then, the 'magic bullet' has had numerous medical or pseudo-medical uses. It seems to have gained renewed prominence in the early years of the AIDS epidemic, when it was naturally assumed that a cure was just around the corner. Not for the first time, however, experts were soon shaking their heads sorrowfully and announcing that there would, in fact, be 'no magic bullet'.

Beyond that, it has come to stand for any quick solution to a problem, whether technical or social. People spent an awful lot of time looking for a 'magic bullet' for millennium syndrome, which was supposed to bring the world to its knees at midnight on 31 December 1999. In the event, it didn't seem to be needed.

The 'magic bullet' as panacea is not the only version, however. Conspiracy theorists will know it as the name given to the single projectile that caused seven separate wounds during the assassination of John F. Kennedy. The sheer unlikeliness of this has made it the most famous projectile since the arrow that felled King Harold. Oliver Stone made a whole film about it.

But what is a 'magic bullet'? Perhaps it is an update of the old 'silver bullet', which supposedly had the power to kill werewolves and vampires. Interestingly, 'silver bullets' are often preferred to 'magic bullets' in America, but there the image owes less to Lon Chaney than to the Lone Ranger, for whom they were a calling card.

Manic

'Did you have a good time last night?' you hear people ask. 'Yeah!' comes the reply. 'It was manic.' They mean it was enjoyable. They are probably not suggesting that it was characterized by extreme excitement, delusions and hallucinations.

Like 'mad', 'manic' is used these days to express simple enthusiasm. Unlike 'mad', 'manic' is still in everyday use as a psychiatric term. Here it characterizes anything associated with mania and anyone suffering from it. Mania has been a word for extreme mental derangement since the fifteenth century. Its origins, beyond Ancient Greek, are shared with similar-sounding words such as 'mind' and 'mental'.

Today it is often used, and misused, in the combination 'manic-depressive'. People say they are 'manic-depressive' or that they are 'manically depressed' when they mean that they are extremely or habitually depressed. Unfortunately, it doesn't work like that. 'Mania' and 'depression' are opposite moods: a 'manic-depressive' is someone who swings from one mood to the other, in extreme cases omitting to stop in the middle. Some prefer the word 'bipolar', but that sounds like something to do with Sir Ranulph Fiennes.

'Mania' comes in several strengths, from mild ('hypomania') to 'Quick, Nurse, He's Out Of His Bed Again'. But there is a more benign version, which affects groups rather than individuals. Since the eighteenth century, the word 'mania' has been used for great excitement, and particularly for popular crazes.

We may think that 'Beatlemania' or 'Spicemania' could only happen in our own, media-fed, era. Not so. In 1777, 'tulip mania' swept Holland. In 1815, English society was beset by 'Scribbleomania', a craze for drawing.

In 1820, there was even 'Queenomania': not a weirdly prescient interest in the works of Mr Freddie Mercury, but a devotion to Queen Caroline, the wife of George IV who tried unsuccessfully to divorce in defiance of public opinion. 'Manic' enough, by anyone's standards.

Mate

Every so often a company tries to stop its workers being overfamiliar with the customers. For a while, 'mate' and 'love' are banned, in favour of 'sir' and 'madam'. But does it last? No chance, mate.

Such edicts are usually directed at 'darling', 'my love' and 'sweetheart'; not because they are 'sexist' but in case they offend the paying customers. But 'sir' and 'madam' are unwelcome replacements. Although theoretically used between social equals (hence 'Dear Sir . . .'), they both began as terms used when addressing social superiors, and the modern Briton doesn't like that.

Today's social relationships start from a premise of equality, and 'mate' suits that. It arrived in Britain in the late fourteenth century, meaning 'comrade' or 'fellow worker'. It seems to have come from Teutonic words meaning 'with' and 'meat', the idea being that your 'mate' was someone you sat down to eat with.

This attractively democratic notion was strengthened in Australia in the nineteenth and twentieth centuries. In the outback, having a good 'mate' could be a matter of life and death, and the word acquired an almost mystical quality.

As a form of address, the word is recorded as early as 1450, among sailors. 'What ho, mate!' they would shout, as lovers of Captain Pugwash will have noticed. The nautical job description 'Master's mate' is recorded half a century later.

Again, the Australians pushed 'mate' to its limit, making it a universal form for addressing anyone other than an armed policeman, when 'sir' was considered politic.

The Australian influence has helped ensure the survival of the word's colloquial sense here in Britain. In formal use, however, it has long moved on to mean 'half of a breeding pair of animals' or, occasionally, 'spouse'.

The E-popping acid-house fraternity recently made the diminutive 'matey' their own chosen form of address. This was originally favoured by nineteenth-century sailors, a group with whom the dance enthusiasts share nothing, except poor taste in trousers.

Matériel

Like any field of human activity, war has jargon. We have learned that 'collateral damage' is the accidental killing of civilians, and that 'degrading the capability' of a state means smashing its military facilities, at least, to a pulp.

But it is still puzzling that commentators have started to use the French 'matériel' to mean military equipment. It does not seem to have been widely used at the time of the Falklands conflict.

That was the last time Britain had a military emergency of its own; everything since has been at the behest of the Americans, who like the word 'matériel'. They even have an outfit called the US Army Materiel Command – slogan: 'America's Arsenal for the Brave' – and have happily Americanized the word for home consumption, losing the acute accent.

But what about the French? For them, *le matériel* means just about anything 'material': stock, apparatus, plant. It has no special military significance. But in the early nineteenth century, Napoleon's adventurism had briefly made France the centre of all things military. The word was imported into English as half of a contrasting pair of adjectives describing the two facets of any military outfit or operation: *personnel*, meaning 'pertaining to people', and *matériel*, meaning 'pertaining to equipment'.

Both were gleefully adapted by the English as nouns, relating to soldiers and armaments respectively. In the nineteenth century, they were specialist terms, used only in italics or between inverted commas to indicate their foreignness.

In our century, 'personnel' quickly broke free of that to become part of the routine of daily life. But 'matériel' has retained its strangeness, remaining the preserve of the military spokesmen, the specialist correspondents and politicians donning the mantle of statesmanship.

Despite the increasing prominence of the word in the media, it has not yet caught on with armchair strategists and saloon-bar Napoleons. If the world remains as unstable as it has been, however, it will soon be inescapable even in the school playground.

Maven

The word 'maven' is a new arrival on these shores, but it is already proving useful, judging by newspaper references to 'monetary mavens', 'new media mavens', 'mavens of corporate governance' and even 'organic compost mavens'.

'Maven' is usually glossed as 'expert'. It emerged from the Jewish press in America in the 1960s. Usually 'mavin' or 'mayvin' at first, it was a Yiddish word that should properly be spelt *meyvn*. Most Yiddish comes from Germanic sources, but *meyvn* was really a Hebrew word, *mebhin*, meaning 'understanding' or 'one who understands'. *Meyvn* is sometimes defined as 'connoisseur', which explains its route into English. Some time in 1965, regular advertisements for a brand of pickled herring appeared in Jewish magazines, with this slogan: 'Tell them the beloved mavin sent you'.

New Yorkers were intrigued, as were other advertisers who mimicked and parodied the series. Eventually it reached parts of the world where the pickled herring is still relatively unknown.

Today the word is popular with journalists, mainly because it provides a replacement for the overworked 'expert'. It is also a common brand name for pieces of computer software that claim a measure of intelligence: there is a 'Crossword Maven', for instance, and a 'File Maven' that applies its expertise to unravelling the mysteries (or miseries) of Microsoft Windows. Interestingly, Jewish writers and businesses in America have accepted the apparently erroneous spelling. There is even a Jewish-orientated Internet search engine, The Maven.

Over here, people still think that a 'maven' must be female, possibly through confusion with raven-haired women called Mavis. At one stage the most common use of the word was for 'fashion maven', a sort of compliment that has since become a job description. According to an article I once read in the *Telegraph*'s fashion pages, 'mavens' are women who 'give designers inspiration and receive free frocks in return'.

Nice work if you can get it: it certainly beats being a connoisseur of manure.

Mental

Mental

On a daytime fashion programme, a student was given a makeover. Pictured for the first time with new clothes, hair and make-up, she was asked for her verdict. 'It's cool,' she enthused. 'It's mental!'

Clearly, in this girl's mind, the two were synonymous and equally desirable.

Oddly, this took place during a national campaign against the use of pejorative terms for those suffering mental illness. Posters across the country helpfully advised against calling people 'loony', 'mong', 'nutter', 'psycho', 'moron' or 'div'.

The campaign did not, however, have much to say about the use of 'mental' as a term of approbation. That might have clouded the issue.

Fundamentally, 'mental' means 'pertaining to the mind'. It meant that when it arrived in English from French in the fifteenth century. The root is the Latin noun *mens*, for mind.

A welter of compound terms followed: mental phenomena, the mental life, mental attitudes, mental development. They were analytical rather than pejorative. Even such expressions as 'mental derangement', coined in 1794, referred to a condition rather than individuals.

But all that changed with the twentieth century and the arrival of eugenics, when these scientific terms were turned into labels and attached to 'mental defectives', 'mental patients' and 'mental cases'.

The blunt epithet 'mental' is recorded first in a 1927 novel by Dorothy L. Sayers, in a discussion by two nurses. J.B. Priestley, writing three years later, has a character 'going mental'. Both were common terms of playground abuse as late as the 1960s.

As attitudes changed, in the 1970s, 'mental' seemed likely to disappear. It was revived by the children of the 1960s, now grown up as punks, heavy metal fans and the like, to describe the wilder headbangers in their number.

The more extreme the behaviour, the more applause it attracted, encouraging young people today to use 'mental' as a synonym for 'great'. They want their heads looking at.

Minging

Tight-knit, isolated groups often develop private dialects – even when that is the only private thing about them.

When the bickering, bored participants of Channel Four's *Big Brother* – the television sensation of 2000 – weren't taking off their clothes, massaging one another or plotting, they were declaring everything 'minging'. Or, more accurately, 'mingin'', which rhymes with 'ringin''.

The word came with Anna, the so-called 'skateboarding nun' from Ireland, who provided ample opportunity for us to hear its context. Everything bad that happened to Anna was 'mingin''. Soon everyone else felt the same way.

Anna's Irishness, though, is a false trail. 'Minging' is Scottish. The verb 'to ming', means 'to stink', both literally and figuratively. Why? Perhaps it has something to do with the Latin *mingere*, to urinate.

Jonathon Green's slang dictionary dates the word only from the 1970s. The earliest example I have found comes from 1991, when it was used by Rab C. Nesbitt, the string-vested Glaswegian philosopher. It has been used most often, and most literally, by Scots, but completeness requires me to note that an article in the *Eastern Daily Press* in 1993 claimed it as a Norfolk dialect term, meaning 'to knead bread'. Sorry, Norfolk, not this time.

Lovers of popular song will have relished the word's appearance in Oasis's 1995 b-side *Round Are [sic] Way*, an illiterate stumble down memory lane. It notes that 'Round are way the birds are minging'. Either someone should call the RSPCA or Noel needs a better rhyme for 'singing'. Stephen Sondheim won't be losing any sleep, that's for sure.

But even before *Big Brother*, a different television cult favoured the word: Ali G, satirical embodiment of white suburbia's desire to be black and cool. Mr G no doubt would like to think he found the word 'minging' while 'hanging' with his homeboys. But his creator, Sacha Baron-Cohen, is just as likely to have stumbled over it at Cambridge: the word is a favourite with students.

Network

Woman: 'I've been trying to network. But my network's got holes in it.' [Laughter]

Man: 'Aren't networks supposed to?' [More laughter]

When a word crops up in a radio sitcom featuring Prunella Scales, you can be sure its radical days are over. And so it proves with the verb 'to network'.

A 'network' *is* supposed to be full of holes. It means something 'in the form of a net', meaning a mesh of rope used for catching things. 'Net' is an ancient word, traceable back to the Common Teutonic of the Dark Ages.

The English noun 'network' is recorded first in the Geneva Bible of 1560. In Exodus, God tells Moses to build an altar, with a 'grate like network of brass'. Moses did his best. Later it came to mean net-shaped natural structures like blood vessels and river systems. Finally it was used to describe invisibly linked processes and relationships.

Now the noun has become a verb, thanks to technology and the social sciences. In the early twentieth century, a group of linked radio stations was called a network, and broadcasters hoped 'to network' their shows. Engineers struggled 'to network' equipment.

But that verb takes an object: you 'network' things. The modern intransitive verb only arrived when working women sought out others like themselves. 'I'm off to network, darling,' they would say. 'Your dinner's in the dog.'

This 'network' had roots in academic musings about 'kinship networks' and 'social networks'. From academia came feminism. When the National Organization of Women split, in 1975, the renegades called themselves a 'network'.

By 1980, however, the word was more business suit than boiler suit. The new networking is epitomized by Mary Scott Welch's 1980 book of the same name, with its hints on gathering business cards. Enter the intransitive verb: 'This book will show you how to network,' it promised.

The 'you' here was clearly female. Men don't 'network', except accidentally, while playing golf.

Nitty-gritty

When I heard that the expression 'nitty-gritty' had been placed on a list of offensive language, I was intrigued, before concluding that the story was some kind of urban myth. But it seems genuinely to have happened, and more than once.

The suggestion is that 'nitty-gritty' refers in some way to the sexual abuse of female slaves aboard ship, and hence is offensive to women, especially black women. Which it would be, if it were true.

The list itself seems to have been drawn up as part of 'equal opportunities awareness' training in a college in the north, although in the way of these things the list seems to have been picked up and used elsewhere. In one newspaper's account, the college was using it in a course for police officers.

When questioned, the list's creators came out fighting. 'I would seriously question the motives of those who criticize our attempts to educate officers on how to identify and thus avoid inappropriate language,' said one, with the boldness often associated with anonymity.

Well, question away. If you are going to start remodelling the language, it pays to be right. 'Nitty-gritty' *is* a black thing, in origin. But it's American, not British, and is unknown before the 1950s, when slavery in the accepted sense of the word had long been abolished. When it does turn up, meaning 'the basics', 'the essentials', 'the harsh reality', it does so in a rather proud and forceful way. It is particularly associated with songs and slogans in the heroic years of black struggle.

As for what it means . . . Well, some say it's just a repetitive play on 'gritty'. More contentiously, Nigel Rees, the broadcaster and writer on language, says that it was a term used by black people about the 'gritty nits' they struggled with when their living accommodation didn't stretch to running water. This is, however, a long way from female slaves in the bottom of ships.

Onside

When Labour MPs are behaving themselves, they are no longer 'on-message' but 'onside'. Perhaps the batteries in their pagers are flat.

On the face of it, the new word is a sporting metaphor, probably coined by Alastair Campbell, the Prime Minister's spokesman and Burnley supporter. He, it seems, is the author of most of New Labour's jargon.

In football, rugby, hockey, gridiron, Australian rules and just about anything else involving a ball and goals, 'onside' means simply 'not offside'. The 'offside' rule was the stroke of anonymous genius that turned association football, for instance, from a chaotic brawl played by violent peasants into the, er, sophisticated intellectual entertainment we know today.

This is not the place for an explanation of the rule, except to say that a player who is 'offside' is in an illegal position and unable to do anything constructive. Whereas someone who is 'onside' can do anything from scoring a goal or a try to turning up to vote the right way when told to do so. The idea of the 'side', meaning one set of participants in a battle or a sporting event – or some cross between the two – turned up in the fourteenth century, although the word itself is much older.

And yet, sport may not be the source of the jargon. There is another remote possibility: in some card games, apparently, a card is 'onside' if it is in a hand when a finesse – winning a trick with a low card – is undertaken. So the loyal Labour MPs could be playing a key role in a metaphorical card game, rather than occupying a house of cards. But that hardly convinces.

The most likely explanation, unfortunately, is also the most mundane. It would seem to be simply a shortened form of 'on our side', a class of Labour MP that our Labour Government occasionally has trouble identifying.

Outlet

What do publicans call pubs? Wayside hostelries, homes-from-home, safe havens in a hostile world? No. They tend to call them 'outlets'.

That's what their bosses call them too. Many publicans are just managers of one branch of a retail drinks chain. To the retailing managers and brand managers of the leisure conglomerates – formerly known as breweries – pubs are simply one 'outlet' for their products. There are also off-licences, supermarkets, corner shops and even petrol stations.

But it's hard not to feel that 'outlet', used for everything from betting shops to public libraries, contains a note of contempt for those queuing up to consume. Surely an 'outlet' is what you have at the end of a sewage pipe?

That is indeed a common use, but the shopping connection has been with us a very long time. The very first 'outlets' were narrow waterways connecting a small body of water to a larger one, and thus offering a means of escape. It is used that way in Richard Hakluyt's *Voyages* of 1600.

Those who persist in hearing something repellent in the word can take strength from Budd's *Diseases of the Liver*, published in 1845, which declares: 'The abscess, if large, may discharge through more outlets than one.'

But from the 1920s on, the expression has been a favourite of the commercial world. As early as 1933, planners were considering 'retail outlets'. It was the respectable *Listener*, in 1966, that described libraries as 'outlets for the distribution of reading matter'. Let us hope that included a note of irony. Lately our retail experience has been enriched by 'factory outlets' imported from America.

There are other senses, none particularly prominent except the psychological. It has been common for at least three centuries to speak of the need for an 'outlet' for dangerous emotions: a wild sense of humour, or excessive energy, or crippling stress. Nowadays, of course, we can go shopping. Or to the pub.

Pester

There has been much discussion of 'pester power'. That's the mysterious force that causes children to erupt at the supermarket checkout if you don't buy them tinned pasta in the shape of *Bob the Builder*.

Parents might guess that 'pester' was related to 'pestilence', not least since *la peste* is French for plague. Plausible, but false. 'Pester' is said to be short for 'empester' or 'impester', which is almost as bad.

The late Latin noun from which it ultimately derives, *pastorium*, means a shackle for a horse. To 'impester' or 'pester' was to entangle and prevent from moving. In Holinshed's *Chronicles*, for instance, written in the sixteenth century, we learn that the Romans were 'pestered with their heavy armour and weapons'.

Crowds were said to have the same paralysing effect, as were vermin to animals. But by the end of the sixteenth century, the word was settling down to something like its present meaning. Here's a phrase from a letter from the Countess of Essex, dated 1600: 'I . . . had never ceased to pester you with my complaints.'

Nowadays the word is almost the property of children, thanks to the journalistic alliteration of 'pester power'. But the phrase was not the invention of journalists.

It came to prominence in the 1990s. A *Guardian* article at the start of the decade, about the jargon of advertising agencies, was the first to give it wide circulation. Advertising people, by the way, took a different view of 'pester power': they thought it was a service they could offer their clients.

They did not invent it either. The earliest reference I can find is from 1979, when the phrase featured in a film called *Kids for Sale*, produced by an American group called Action for Children's Television. At that stage, they'd already been campaigning for ten years against the disruption caused by advertising aimed at children.

They didn't stop it. They didn't even slow it. But at least they gave us a name for it.

Pixilated

Pixilated

'Becki came on the phone,' said the American. 'She was clearly pixilated.' From the context, it was obvious he meant drunk. But why?

In Britain we use the verb 'to pixilate', but only in a technical sense. An image is 'pixilated' if it is broken up into dots or squares, as on a television or computer screen. Those are the 'pixels', derived from *pix els* or 'picture elements'. The abbreviation is from the 1960s, but 'picture elements' were mentioned in the 1920s, when television involved shining a bright light through a spinning disk.

The most obviously 'pixilated' human beings are those on *Crimewatch* whose faces have been turned into a mosaic of coloured rectangles to hide their identities. Being horribly blurred like that is certainly suggestive of being drunk, or perhaps hungover. The association is helped by the word's initial 'pix . . .', not unlike that other well-known word for drunk.

But that's a false trail. The American 'pixilated' is found well before television. In 1840s New England it meant whimsical, confused or slightly mad. Literally, 'pixilated' meant 'under the influence of pixies', who were notorious for leading people astray. 'Pixie-led' was a synonym. 'Away with the fairies,' as we might say.

The meaning is current: American newspapers have been known to refer to 'Shakespeare's pixilated *Midsummer Night's Dream*'. Mostly, though, 'pixilated' means 'intoxicated'.

And how did pixies get to America? A pixie (or piskie) is a West Country variant of the fairy, found in Devon and Cornwall especially, and first recorded in the early seventeenth century. But the early English settlers of New England were from the East of England, where the pixie was unknown.

Mind you, the presence of pixies in the West Country is a mystery in itself. The word is said to be Swedish in origin, which suggests that some Viking had gone badly astray. Perhaps he'd been drinking.

Platform

Once, a 'platform' was a flat surface, raised above the ground. Then it came to mean the standpoint of a political party. And now? Just about anything.

It means, among other things: the floorpan shared by a range of cars; a system of computer hardware; a computer operating system; anything, from mobile phone to 'set-top box', that provides access to digital television or the Internet; a genre of computer game; a glorified website intended to assist businesses.

And those are just today's meanings. More will have arrived by tomorrow.

In origin, a 'platform' is the fifteenth-century French *platte fourme*, a 'flat shape'. When adopted by English in the 1550s, the shapes were geometrical figures or architectural floorplans. Soon it meant the floor itself; and then any flat surface. Hamlet, for instance, meets his father's ghost 'on the platform'. Not alongside the 'up' line at Elsinore South, you understand, but on a level part of the fortifications.

Later the word was used for raised wooden surfaces, and, when the railways came, for the flat bed of a wagon. Hence the motor car 'platform' – and the dangerously tempting entrance to a Routemaster bus. Stations only acquired 'platforms' later, in the 1840s.

Political speakers have stood on 'platforms' since the early nineteenth century. When they agreed, they would share the 'platform'; and soon the word began to mean a set of policies.

But what about those computers? Aircraft and spacecraft have gyroscopically controlled guidance 'platforms'. The PR companies who promoted these devices won the job of pushing the first microcomputers in the early 1980s. Tired of the word 'computer', they borrowed the aerospace term.

It turned into a metaphor. A computer 'platform' is a stage upon which you, your software or your business can perform. Mobile phones, the Internet and so on also provide a 'platform', while being no more interesting in themselves than the bare stage at Stratford – or the place where you wait for the delayed 18.18 to Dartford.

Plural

People leaving powerful jobs in business sometimes give strange reasons. But the City was taken aback when people started talking about 'going plural'.

To be 'plural' suggests becoming more than one person. Good for time management, admittedly, but scary. Think of Dr Jekyll and Mr Hyde, or poor Sybil, her sixteen assorted personalities trapped inside the body of Sally Field.

But to those captains of industry who favoured it, 'going plural' just meant doing several jobs. Just like many of their former employees, in fact, but without the element of grinding financial necessity. 'Going plural is very exciting,' said one. 'No one else has really done it.'

'Plural' is really a grammatical term, used about words rather than things. It comes from the Old French *plurel*, an adjectival form of *plus*, and arrived here in the fourteenth century, when it featured in considerations of the Trinity. Is God singular or plural?

Only in the mid-nineteenth century did it achieve wider use, usually in dressing up unpalatable ideas. In 1860, John Stuart Mill proposed 'plural voting', a euphemism for extra votes for the educated. Shortly afterwards, the Mormons of Utah invented 'plural marriage' as a euphemism for polygamy. At various times since, others have advocated 'plural societies' or 'plural democracy', both of which can mean racial segregation.

'Going plural' cropped up abroad in the 1980s as a political slogan. But as a career plan, it is our own, attributed to Sir Peter Parker, one-time boss of British Rail, who is supposed to have espoused it in the 1970s.

It came into its own when for the first time people faced a future without jobs for life. In 1992, the accountants KPMG issued a booklet promoting the idea. It featured a man who counsels drug addicts during the week, then earns a few bob at the weekend making videos of weddings.

A couple of good ideas there for those City bosses. Someone should send them a copy.

Portal

How should you react if a group of teenage 'entreprenerds' invite you to take a look at their 'portal'? Tell them you're not a good sailor? Ask whether a 'portal' is more like a porpoise or a turtle? Or give them your life savings?

Those enjoying Britain's struggle with e-commerce – a kind of Ealing dot.comedy – will know that a 'portal' is a sort of door through which people enter the Internet. As they pass through, those manning the 'portal' attempt to extract money from them. At least, that's the theory.

Before becoming a metaphorical gateway, a 'portal' was a real entrance. Derived from the Latin *porta*, and turning up in fourteenth-century English, it meant something smarter than a mere door. Later it came to mean the valves of the heart, the entrance to a hermit's cave and the point where a malevolent germ enters the human body.

'Portal', in the Internet context, has slightly poetic associations. It suggests that the Internet user is entering on a heroic but reassuringly old-fashioned adventure: 'Who chortles at the portal of Myrtle the Immortal?' Such 'portals' should guard fabulous palaces, ornate temples and gloomy monastic libraries.

Today's 'portals' like to suggest they are the entrance to a shopping mall. But the Internet is not much like that: people go for a look, but many leave their wallets at home.

'Portal' found its way into Internet language because it had already had a couple of outings as an acronym in the world of information technology. The first was a computer language. The second was something called 'Private Offerings, Resales and Trading Through Automated Linkages'.

This was an American initiative that removed much of the paperwork used in American share trading. It was put in place after the Wall Street crash to keep a brake on things. Without it, private investors could trade instantly. And they certainly do: no PORTAL, no 'portals', no dotcom boom – and bust.

Posse

What is a 'posse'? An armed band of frontiersmen in pursuit of an outlaw? A gang of malevolent youths? Or a group of sycophants, hired by radio DJs to laugh at their jokes, endure their sarcasm and make them feel important? Answer: all three.

Once, DJs were locked in an empty studio, alone with a pile of records. Now the studio is full of people. No wonder the licence fee keeps rising.

This 'posse' idea – sometimes called the 'zoo' format – is usually attributed to Steve Wright, who developed it in his Radio One days. Chris Evans, Zoe Ball and the rest all imitated it. Even dear old Wogan has a sidekick or two.

When Wright referred to his wise-cracking coterie as his 'posse', he was making a witty reference to the teenage gangs of South London. They, in turn, had taken the term from the murderous youth of Los Angeles.

Where did the American gangs find it? Presumably in Westerns, where a body of angry locals, called the 'posse', is regularly raised by the sheriff. Despite their frontier associations, however, both terms are from English law.

The sheriff was an Anglo-Saxon official, representing royal authority in a county. His powers have been declining since 1066, but for many years he was entitled to raise the *posse comitatus*, a medieval Latin term meaning 'the force of the county'. This was a body of men called together to enforce the law. Anyone refusing faced perpetual servitude and the confiscation of all property. Neighbourhood Watch it was not.

Here, the system died out. But America inherited our legal system and terminology and found the 'posse' ideal for taming the Wild West, since it had the right to use force.

Even today, it is a crime in some US states to refuse to join a 'posse'. In British broadcasting, however, it should be a crime to set one up.

Professional

Have you noticed the way anyone with a white coat and a whiff of disinfectant is now a 'health professional'?

Nurses, physiotherapists, radiographers and so on are keen to acquire the 'professional' aura that once belonged to doctors alone. They should know that the word is not all good news.

A 'profession' is a public declaration: we retain this in the idea of making 'a profession of innocence'. In the thirteenth century, a 'profession' was the declaration you made on entering a religious order. In Tudor times, you made a 'profession' that you knew about one of three branches of learning: medicine, law and religion.

These required a university education, but you could also make a 'profession' of warfare, which was more a matter of aptitude. At the same time, people referred quite happily to such 'professions' as tailoring, haberdashery, cutting hair and thieving, where degrees were optional.

In the nineteenth century, the Top People tried to monopolize the word 'profession'. As they did so, music-hall wits gleefully undermined them by applying it ironically to the callings of criminals, tramps and actors. And then, in 1888, Kipling declared that prostitution was the 'oldest profession'. He did not provide evidence.

The adjective 'professional' now began to be used disparagingly of those who did for money what other people did for love, among them sportsmen and musicians. The complaint was that they were not sincere: we say the same today of 'professional cockneys' and 'professional seducers'.

In our own time, we have the 'professional foul', in which a footballer hacks a man down to prevent a goal, thereby furthering his club at the expense of the sport. Once condoned by players and commentators, it is now frowned upon. 'Professional', once implying grudging admiration, has become interchangeable with 'cynical'.

To say someone is 'professional' recognizes their efficiency and technical excellence, but it may cast doubt on their sincerity and ethics. If that's what 'health professionals' want, good luck to them.

Project

When history looks back on the last few years, what will it make of the 'New Labour project'?

That 'project' is a strangely flattering word to apply to the pursuit and preservation of political power. It has a heroic note, hinted at in this American definition, from the *Webster-Merriam Dictionary*: 'A planned undertaking,' it says, and then elaborates. 'A large, usually government-supported, undertaking.'

It is worth noting that John F. Kennedy used the word when he launched the Apollo mission. 'No single space project in this period will be more impressive to mankind, or more important for the long-range exploration of space.' The first part was right.

Those who glorify politicians have borrowed a little of this technocratic glamour, even if they only use it to describe such valuable tasks as making Labour MPs take up suits and throw off socialism, or, in the case of the subsequent 'Hague project', getting Tory MPs to 'bond' without recourse to industrial adhesives.

Politicians should be aware that 'project' is an adaptation of the Latin *projectum*, which means not only 'thrown forward' but 'thrown out'.

When it first appeared in English, in the fifteenth century, a 'project' meant a plan, on paper. Our modern sense arrived in the early seventeenth century, when people first began to put together vague and far-fetched 'projects', without paperwork, and looked for other people to pay for them.

The political use is more modern. There is a definition in the *OED*, from 1952, that almost matches: 'a co-operative enterprise, often with a social or scientific purpose, but also in industry, etc.' Only that word 'co-operative' seems out of place. Before that there was the wartime Manhattan Project, which mixed pure science with heavy engineering and ended up saving democracy.

History may conclude, however, that the 'New Labour project' is more like the 'projects' we all did at school, when the secret was to concentrate on presentation in the hope that the content would be overlooked.

Pukka

Pukka

When the chef Jamie Oliver first appeared on the television he looked about fifteen. But he had an oddly antique vocabulary. Not only was everything in his kitchen 'wicked' and 'crucial', it was also 'pukka'.

'Pukka' means 'authentic' or 'genuine', although young Jamie used it simply as a term of approval. It is quite unusual these days, cropping up mainly in old-fashioned contexts where no one feels embarrassed by its imperial overtones. You see it in the City pages and in sports reports. You used to hear it a lot in *It Ain't Half Hot Mum*, one of the few programmes the BBC seems reluctant to repeat.

As all of this suggests, 'pukka' is an Anglo-Indian term, derived from the Hindi *pakka* and appearing first in English at the end of the seventeenth century. The Hindi word means 'mature', 'cooked' or 'solid'.

It was often balanced by its opposite, *cutcha*, meaning 'raw' or 'unripe', notably in local systems of weights, which came in two versions, the 'pakka' and the 'cutcha', just as we once had pounds troy and pounds avoirdupois and now pints and litres on the same supermarket shelves.

For building, mud and timber were 'cutcha' materials, whereas kiln-fired bricks and mortar were 'pakka'. Similarly, permanent things and people came to be called 'pakka' or 'pukka'. In the nineteenth and twentieth centuries, it spread across the English-speaking world, like pyjama and bungalow, but unlike them it has never totally lost its subcontinental aura.

It tends to be used faintly ironically, for its historical connotations: people might praise an Indian restaurant for its 'pukka' food, or suggest that someone born on a tea plantation would bring 'pukka' management to a tarnished organization.

Sometimes you read that someone whose speech is redolent of the old BBC Empire Service has a 'pukka accent'. No one would make that mistake about Jamie Oliver, however. He seems to have taken elocution lessons from Mick Jagger.

Rapt

'Go and tell your mother,' says Dad, hearing about some teenage triumph. 'She'll be rapt.'

Would that be 'rapt' as in 'fully absorbed or intent, enraptured'? Or 'carried away with feeling or lofty thought'? Not really. It helps to know that we're in Australia, where 'rapt' is both more common and less dramatic than those English definitions suggest. Not so much 'transported by emotion' as 'quite pleased'.

'Rapt' appears every day in *Neighbours*, the antipodean soap opera enjoyed by everyone from Oxford dons to underemployed writers. It is a favourite in the Australian press too, where it makes for punchy headlines. And when Aussies win at sport, they are invariably 'rapt': you'd think they'd be used to it by now.

'Rapt' is still considered slang, which is why it is mainly found among sports personalities and the young. But it is also common in New Zealand, and catching on here and in the US, where exotic new expressions are highly prized.

The *Australian National Dictionary* stores 'rapt' under 'wrapped', which is showing its age. It finds it first in a novel of 1963: 'She's wrapped in me', meaning obsessed or infatuated. By the 1970s, 'wrapped' stood alone. 'I don't think she was wrapped,' it quotes, meaning 'pleased'. The new spelling arrived with the 1980s.

Spelt 'rapt', it is the English word, taken from the Latin *raptus*, meaning seized. In the fifteenth century, 'rapt' meant 'taken bodily to heaven'. Some Christian groups look forward to 'The Rapture', meaning the day when God comes to collect the faithful, dead or alive.

In English, 'rapt with' and 'wrapped up in' can both mean obsessed. The Australian dictionary says its 'wrapped' (or 'rapt') is a blend of the two. But there's another possibility.

In Australia, to 'rap' someone, oddly, is to praise them. A person who has been 'rapped' would probably feel quite pleased. Hence 'rapt'. Would they enter a different state of consciousness? Only in *Neighbours*.

Raunchy

These are fine times for television viewers who love great literature. Since producers discovered that the heroines of the nineteenth-century classics occasionally take their clothes off, costume dramas have never been more popular.

To quote a typical Channel Four announcement: 'And now, the first of four remarkable and raunchy episodes of . . . *Anna Karenina*.'

'Raunchy'? It makes the poor woman sound like Geri Halliwell: but then, that was probably the point.

'Raunchy' today means sexy, provocative and earthy. It was popularized in the 1960s in the States, when performers like Janis Joplin seemed to have it as a middle name. By the 1970s it had spread across the English-speaking world, giving rise to such variants as 'raunchiness' and 'raunch', sometimes used as a synonym for pornography.

But where did it come from? It is recorded first in a 1939 magazine article about an Air Force cadet camp in America, where drill lasted an hour for those who were good and three for those who were 'raunchy'. A curious image, unless you know that in those days 'raunchy' carried no innuendo. It simply meant sloppy or scruffy.

Other early synonyms were: incompetent, unpleasant, contemptible, mean, disreputable and grubby. *American Speech*, the journal of the American Dialect Society, said in 1968 that 'raunchy' generally meant 'stinky, grubby, scabby, dirty or cheap'. How quickly that changed.

But what are the word's origins? There is a word 'ranchy', first spotted in 1903 in the States in a reference to a 'flea-ranchy' old monk, and confidently glossed as 'dirty, disgusting, indecent'. Perhaps becoming 'ranchy' or 'raunchy' was something that happened when you worked on a ranch?

Sadly, scholarly support for this view is lacking. 'Raunchy' may come from 'rancid', or from a dialect use of 'raunch' to mean 'raw'. Or perhaps from the Italian *rancio*, meaning 'rancid' or 'rotten'.

Either way, it's not quite Tolstoy's idea of *Anna Karenina*.

Re-engineering

Of all management terms, none is more alarming than 're-engineering'. Most of us fear that one person's 're-engineering' is another's 're-dundancy'.

It has had this implication from the start. The first recorded use, in America in 1944, was in a discussion about how jobs that had been 're-engineered' – adapted, modified or reorganized – for women during the war could be given back to men.

We took up the word at the same time, but in its literal sense: we talked about 're-engineering' aerials and electrical components. It is still sometimes used in this way, but generally 're-engineering' is a process businesses undergo when they swallow a particular brand of American snake oil.

This 're-engineering' reflects the fact that the locals have long used the word 'engineering' to mean 'making something happen'. In the nineteenth century, they talked about people 'engineering' bills through Congress or 'engineering' a trade dispute. We followed suit, in such expressions as 'I'm hoping to engineer an encounter in the stationery room.'

All of which drives actual engineers round the bend. To them it is part of a climate of imprecision in which almost everyone is an engineer, from the person who nails your Sky dish to the wall to the person who puts the 'non-dairy whitener' in the coffee machine.

But engineers have played many roles over the centuries. In the Middle Ages, they were people who built fortifications and 'engines' of war, before turning to canals and railways as 'civil' engineers. At the time of Shakespeare, however, the word meant anyone ingenious, particularly an inventor or a plotter.

Most commonly, the word means a maker or operator of machines, or engines, particularly steam engines. In America, an engineer is a train driver.

Our university-educated engineers would prefer things the way they are in Germany, where an engineer is addressed as Herr Doktor, if not Herr Professor. But then, most people in Germany are.

Relaxed

In politics, it is always important to be 'relaxed'.

When Peter Mandelson was Trade and Industry Secretary, he declared that New Labour was 'intensely relaxed about people getting filthy rich'. Then, when Mandelson was sacked over an undisclosed home loan, Gordon Brown indicated that he was 'relaxed' about his press officer leaking the story that brought him down.

But these people are not 'relaxed' in the way we would be. By 'relaxed' they mean 'in agreement' – even 'happy'.

Usually to be 'relaxed' is to be at ease. As the *Cassell Dictionary of Clichés* points out, it has replaced 'tanned and fit' as the standard description of a celebrity returning from somewhere sunny, or a fugitive dragged back from the Costa Del Crime.

To 'relax' comes from the Latin *relaxare*, to loosen. In English, from the seventeenth century, it was used for the slackening of muscles in animals and humans. Inevitably, to 'relax' came to mean to lose grip, something that afflicted laws, religions and governments. As a son of the manse, Gordon Brown at least will know that 'relaxed', has, in the past, meant anything from broad-minded to sinful.

By the nineteenth century, to 'relax' began to suggest a calm state of mind, signalled by a loosening of one's rigid posture and facial expression. In our own century, though, it has become a purely psychological phenomenon: it means we have shed anxiety. 'Relaxing' things are highly prized: hence the unceasing efforts of Classic FM to present the intellectual peaks of Western musical culture as 'smooth classics', a kind of aural tranquillizer.

To be 'relaxed' in the political sense is to be more than tolerant. When we were told that Mr Brown was 'relaxed' about his spokesman's activities, we were supposed to think that he allowed them to happen – but no more.

To believe that, however, you would have to have a rather 'relaxed' grip on reality.

Rock

To say something 'rocks' is to praise it highly, particularly in America. 'Geology rocks!' you might say, if you were out of your mind.

Oddly, the one thing that doesn't 'rock' for many young people is 'rock music'. But while they may not buy the records, 'rock' remains a dominant cultural force among American baby boomers, their children and their grandchildren.

'It rocks!' sounds like an expression from the 1970s, the era of expressionist hair, triple albums and forty-minute guitar solos. But it has actually been with us a bit longer, as long as jazz, in fact.

The verb 'to rock' comes from the Old English *roccian*, meaning to push a baby in a cradle. But, like jazz, not all its connotations are as innocent. In black American speech the word had a strong sexual component that crossed into music. As early as 1922, there was a song called 'My Man Rocks Me (With One Steady Roll)' which seems unlikely to have been concerned with the bakery trade.

Cab Calloway used the expression 'rock me', along with a certain amount of gibberish, in his brilliant 'Hi de Ho' of 1938. And in the jazz press of the 1930s, pundits who said a tune 'rocks' were praising it highly.

When 'rock 'n' roll' arrived, in the early 1950s, it wasn't called that. It began as a harsh, grown-up music, played and sung by black people and labelled 'race' or 'rhythm and blues'. But when New York DJ Alan Freed started promoting it to white people, and white people started to sing and play it, he looked for a new name without racial connotations.

Overt sexual connotations were presumably less of a problem, since the phrase Freed found was 'rock 'n' roll', which had already appeared in a couple of decidedly raunchy songs.

Well, that's ancient history. History rocks! But what about the music? Sadly, modern kids tend to leave that kind of thing to Grandpa.

Savvy

'Savvy': what a versatile little word. It can be a noun ('Applicants must have the necessary savvy'), adjective ('Are you savvy with this system?'), or verb ('Do it now. Savvy?').

Many of us know 'savvy' best as a verb, because it used to turn up in the warlike comics we read as children. In every edition, a clean-cut British hero would capture a group of untrustworthy 'sausage-eaters' or 'square-heads'. 'Don't make a move,' he'd snarl. 'Savvy?'

This, we were led to believe, meant 'Do you understand?' in all known languages. Hence our vast international reputation as linguists.

Oddly enough, though, that's approximately what it does mean. The *OED* notes that it has existed since 1785 in what it calls 'Negro-Eng' or 'Pigeon-Eng' (sic). It is thought to originate in the Spanish *sabe usted?* meaning 'Do you know?', although some feel it derives from the French *savez vous?* Both are descendants of the Latin *sapere*, to be wise.

The *OED*, which predates political correctness, gives a couple of charming examples from the nineteenth century, including this bit of supposed Caribbean speech from *The Life of a Planter in Jamaica*: 'Dey hab not savey dat de storekeeper hab be deir broder Joseph.'

Recently, noun and adjective versions have enjoyed something of a vogue, having re-emerged from America. The Americans use 'savvy' as a noun in various compounds to indicate experience, know-how and shrewdness. They speak of 'business savvy' or 'political savvy'.

The adjective, meanwhile, has found a niche in the computer world. Here, though, it is not only people who can be 'savvy', meaning intelligent or wise, but things. You see computer programs described as 'gimp-savvy' or 'Linux savvy', meaning that they will work within those particular programs or software environments.

It is also a handy component in website names. You won't have to look far to find 'savvyshopper', 'homesavvy', 'savvymotoring' and 'savvytraveller'. The latter offers plenty of opportunities to try your language skills. Savvy?

— YOUR GOSSIP OR YOUR LIFE.

Scam

Scam

The campaign to keep English British took a mortal blow the day Neil Carter in *The Archers* was heard to accuse Eddy Grundy of carrying out a 'scam'. What next? Clive Horrobin being run to ground by 'the Feds'?

Such vocabulary would once have left listeners mystified, but these days the little word is common. That is partly because it is a boon to headline writers trying to sum up any number of fiddles, cons and rackets. It doesn't necessarily imply a crime, so local papers find it the perfect word when the tea money goes missing at the bowls club.

In America, where the word emerged, the 'scams' – fiddles, cons, rackets – tend to be bigger and better. When it first emerged, in the early 1960s, it applied particularly to fraudulent bankruptcies. But 'scam' had other nuances. It also meant inside information or gossip, preferably damaging in nature. Thus Neil might conceivably have asked, 'What's the scam on Caroline?' But Neil's not like that.

It seems possible to pinpoint the word's breakthrough in this country. In 1976, a band called Steely Dan released a record entitled *The Royal Scam*, the title track referring to the experiences of Hispanic immigrants in the USA. The meaning of the title was discussed at length, and the word entered the British version of the language. A few sophisticates, of course, claimed they had already encountered it, in crime fiction.

It certainly found an easy acceptance, and there may be an explanation for that. Some dictionaries claim that 'scam' derives from our own 'scamp', which seems absurd. But they do sound similar.

We apply 'scamp', in a friendly, indulgent way, to a naughty child. But in origin it was harsher. An eighteenth-century 'scamp' was a highway robber. A dictionary of 1825 defined it as a 'fellow devoid of honour and principle'. The kind of person to carry out a 'scam', in fact, and not very far from Eddy Grundy.

Segue

A magazine article tells us that an actress started in theatre, but 'soon segued to television and film . . .' Now what could that mean? Waltzed off? Resigned herself? Declared undying allegiance?

It helps to know that 'segue' is pronounced seg-way, indicating that its provenance is not English or French but Italian. What is being described here is a kind of musical transition, and the international language of music is Italian.

'Segue' is the third person singular of *seguire*, to follow, and means 'it follows'. It is a direction to the performer, indicating that he or she move straight to the next section without a break for applause, a change of shirt or a couple of pints with the brass section, who are already in the pub.

There is nothing new about using 'segue' in this sense. Italian has been the basic tool for writing down musical expression since the seventeenth century. 'Segue' itself is first recorded in an English musical dictionary in 1740. But it is also used as a noun by jazz players, to refer to an example of a seamless transition from one piece to another. 'After the segue,' they say.

In our century it has come to mean other transitions, especially those with a vaguely 'musical' fluidity. Those old enough to have heard Radio One in the 1970s will recall the way DJs prided themselves on the smoothness of their 'segues', by which they meant playing two records in succession without saying anything witless in between. These days, of course, that would be a sacking offence, even on Radio Three.

More recently, however, the word has started to be used of transitions from shot to shot in a film, or even from one way of life to another. In other words, the word itself has 'segued', just like our actress, who, we can now translate, 'made a smooth transition' to TV and film.

Serial

Once, 'serial' was an innocent word. As a noun, it meant a piece of fiction arranged in episodes for magazines, radio or television. As an adjective, it was usually paired with 'number' to create something especially prized by trainspotters, collectors and other obsessives. Boring, but harmless.

Since the early 1990s, though, 'serial' has fallen into bad company, teaming up with 'killer' to form a replacement for that unfashionable term 'mass murderer', which has in turn found new employment in the world of genocide. The sudden fashionability of 'serial killing' in films, books and television drama – not to mention real life – soon made the expression ubiquitous.

Newly famous, 'serial' turned itself into a faintly daring replacement for 'habitual' in a range of new compounds, mostly facetious. As early as 1992, *The Economist* was describing the former Shah of Iran as 'a serial adulterer'. 'Serial dieting', 'serial vomiting', 'serial law-breaking', 'serial dribbling', 'serial farting' and many more soon followed.

All this activity fits the word's primary definition: 'Belonging to, forming part of, or consisting of a series; taking place or occurring in a regular succession.'

'Serial' developed in the nineteenth century as an adjective from 'series', but its ultimate source is the Latin *serere*, to join. It has many technical uses in science, music, education, psychology and linguistics but before the global success of *The Silence of the Lambs* it had never been exactly popular.

That gave it a niche, particularly as a comedy idea. Newspaper columnists applied it particularly to members of the last Tory cabinet, who had to suffer being described as 'serial bunglers' and 'serial adulterers' until the idea faded gently away. But before that it had even made it to Hollywood, in the shape of 1994's *Serial Mom*.

Then a couple of real serial killers turned up on this side of the Atlantic and suddenly no one was seeing the funny side any more.

Shag

Shag

There has been an awful lot of nonsense written about the word 'shag'. But it seems a shame to disappoint.

Now that our language is global – which is to say American – it was delightful when a film called *Austin Powers II: The Spy Who Shagged Me* baffled people all over the States.

We should not exaggerate this. American Anglophiles and lovers of British low comedy (is there any other sort?) knew that the noun 'shag' meant more than it says in their dictionaries: 'a rough surface', 'a fabric with a nap', 'a hopping dance step'. But everyone else had a rude awakening.

'Shag' appears in Old English as *sceacga*, meaning 'hair', leading eventually to all those rough materials and fabrics. And fans of 'The cormorant or common shag / Who lays his eggs in a paper bag' may guess that his name reflects his distinctive hairstyle.

But the verb, and our rude noun, began life as a variant of 'shake'. When Jesus walks on the water, in our Bible, he does so to reach the disciples' boat, 'tossed on the waves'. But in Wycliffe's version, *c.* 1380, the boat is 'shoggid with waves'.

This shaking may have given the Americans their hopping dance of the 1930s and 1940s: the 'shag'. But it led to our current sense much earlier. 'Shag' defined as 'to copulate' appears in Grose's *Dictionary of the Vulgar Tongue* in 1788 and has been with us ever since.

Interestingly, in nineteenth-century Gloucestershire, to 'shag' meant to wander off. This, and another version meaning 'to chase', turned up in America, providing them with even more excuses for failing to understand *The Spy Who Shagged Me*.

The *OED* rarely raises a smile. But I defy anyone to read the lengthy entry for 'shag' without roaring.

Moralists have deplored the crudity of the Austin Powers films: but 'shag' was also used by, for instance, Kingsley Amis. It's another British gift to the world. Perhaps we should cherish it.

Stakeholder

The 'stakeholder' was once the Big Idea of the incoming Labour Government. But it was a Big Idea almost no one understood.

'"Stakeholder society" as a slogan has the considerable disadvantages of being both unattractive and unintelligible,' wrote the *Daily Telegraph* in February 1996, after a particularly damning opinion poll.

So 'stakeholder' was buried, and a succession of Even Bigger Ideas plucked out of the air. But then it came back, as the label on a type of occupational pension: what a comedown.

In the City pages, 'stakeholder' simply means shareholder. But Tony Blair's 'stakeholder economy' – to use the original version – was different. It meant an economy in which 'a part is available to all' or, at least, to those prepared to play their part by working hard and saving for old age.

Where did this particular stick and carrot spring from? Perhaps from Will Hutton's *The State We're In*, a proto-Blairite bestseller of 1995. He may have borrowed the term from the sociologist Ralf Dahrendorf, who used it to say that companies should consider not only shareholders but 'stakeholders', meaning employees, customers and neighbours.

In the Blairite formula, society itself would be similarly responsive to all its 'stakeholders'. They would not, of course, require 'a stake in the country'. That nineteenth-century phrase meant land ownership, and was used to keep the masses away from the ballot box.

Originally, a 'stake' was a sum of money you gambled. A 'stakeholder' held the 'stake' while the gamble took place. But what's the connection with the 'stake' you bang in the ground? That is Old English, but the gambling 'stake' didn't appear until the sixteenth century.

It has been suggested your 'stake' got its name because you had to hang it on a wooden post so people could see it. But this would only work if you were betting your shirt: money would blow away.

Of course, the 'stakeholder pension' includes no element of gambling. Does it?

Sticky

Businesses used to want to be slick. But in the era of e-commerce, the thing to be is 'sticky'.

Management schools are struggling to find the secret of 'stickiness', essential if you want your website to make you a paper billionaire before you get your first grey hair.

Originally, all you needed was 'traffic', meaning people taking a look. Now, though, the site has to be 'sticky', which means people 'stick around' long enough for you to take money from them. Some American sites claim to hold their readers for five hours. Of course, they don't have phone bills – or lives.

The term has been ascribed to Trevor Bentley of the British magazine *Management Accounting*, writing in April 1997, when the World Wide Web was new. 'The stickiness of the WWW . . . may catch many flies, but it is their choice to be there in the first place,' he mused.

The flies are Internet users, lured into a sticky cobweb and held there to be devoured by commercial interests. Today the 'web' analogy is barely mentioned, but 'stickiness' thrives.

To 'stick', originally, was to stab with a sharp implement. Anglo-Saxon writing is full of people being 'sticked' (as they said then). The stabbing, prodding motion is recalled in such phrases as 'Why did you stick your finger into that socket?' or 'Look, it's made your hair stick up!'

'Sticking' these days is mostly about staying still, but the two ideas, stabbing and staying, are related. A sword found 'sticked' or 'stuck' was one that couldn't be moved because its point was embedded in something, usually a body. Glue came later.

To be 'sticky' has not always been a good thing. Since the nineteenth century, 'sticky' people have been difficult. To the undemonstrative soldiers of World War I, a 'sticky' situation was one that was very perilous.

And anyone trying to make a fortune from the Internet should brush up on another early twentieth-century idiom: 'to come to a sticky end'.

Sussed

Old slang never dies: it just finds a new career in marketing. Consider the fate of 'sussed'.

When Marks & Spencer was updating its image, shoppers were met by stark slogans on placards and balloons. Among them was the single word 'Sussed'.

One newspaper reported that this would give the chain 'a little street cred'. But that's tricky. Adjectives like 'sussed', meaning 'streetwise' or 'smart', are much favoured by great institutions trying to talk to the young. But they sound patronizing. The BBC, for instance, used *Sussed* as the name of an earnest youth discussion programme. In 1992, the Consumers' Association launched *Check It Out*, a magazine for 'teenagers' who wanted to be 'sussed and streetwise'. They proved exactly that, giving it a wide berth.

Nonetheless, 'sussed' appeals, because it suggests a person has the kind of practical wisdom you only learn at the School of Hard Knocks. This is explained by the word's origins.

In the 1930s, the criminal fraternity spoke of being picked up 'on sus', meaning 'on suspicion', or 'as a sus', meaning 'as a suspected person'. Under the nineteenth-century 'sus' law, simply being a 'suspected person' was an offence.

That law was abolished in 1981, by which time 'to sus' had established itself as a verb. It is first recorded in 1950s police jargon: 'Who's sussed [suspected] for this job?' Soon it was used outside the criminal context, though in the same milieu. Frank 'Fings' Norman used it in a 1958 book, *Bang to Rights*, where someone 'half sussed [sic]' that someone was making fun of him. To 'suss out', though, is to investigate: that only arrived in the late 1960s.

When M & S 'sussed' that no one was going into its shops, it tried to 'suss out' why. Eventually it declared itself 'sussed', and flattered its customers by suggesting that they were too. But they always have been. It may not be a fashionable business strategy, but who else sells underpants that last as long as the average marriage?

Sustainable

A famous slogan insisted that no one ever got fired for buying IBM. Politicians, planners, environmentalists, educators and pundits have all concluded that they can't go wrong with the word 'sustainable'.

Unknown in its present sense before the 1960s, it is now spreading at a rate that would barely seem 'sustainable' in itself. Today something is 'sustainable' if is capable of carrying on at the same level or – and here the alert will spot an ambiguity – at the same rate of growth.

A fish that just avoids extinction is 'sustainable'. So, apparently, is a housing plan that places 40,000 more ticky-tacky boxes in the British countryside every year. You can see why such a word, with its air of environmental virtue, would please everyone from the Wildlife Trust to the House Builders Federation.

To 'sustain' something is to bear it, either physically or emotionally, from the Old French *sustenir*, meaning 'to hold up from beneath'. It has been with us since the thirteenth century. One minor occupational variant: when reporters say someone 'sustained a broken nose', they are using an American cliché of the 1880s. It made no sense even then.

Something 'sustainable' is something that can be borne, continued or maintained: a population, for instance, or a rate of development. In the nineteenth century, only arguments were 'sustainable', meaning capable of being supported. But in the 1960s, economists invented the idea of 'sustainable growth', a rise in living standards that would continue to rise indefinitely. Politicians seized upon it.

When *Doomwatch* came on the television in the 1970s, and the West discovered environmentalism, attention turned to the idea of 'sustainable' animal populations, weather, minerals, local economies and so on. None proved much of a match for 'sustainable growth', as embraced by the whole world.

Still, never mind, the word has thrived, not least because of its remarkable flexibility. The meanings of words are among the least 'sustainable' of resources.

Tad

'In this image,' writes the author of a book on photo manipulation, 'I used my genuine calibrated eyeball to determine when the apartment building was vertical, and I was just a tad off. (Note: a tad is a Texas unit of measurement. 1 tad = 0.2837 mm, plus or minus a foot.)'

This is a joke, or what passes for one in manuals of computer software: the calibrated eyeball should have alerted you. But it is true that 'tad' is an American expression, and it is about size.

Naturally, it is fashionable here. The *Independent*, for instance, is always telling us that films are 'a tad' slow when it means slightly. In other places, though, it is very much disliked. The *Daily Telegraph* no longer insists that 'only Malays may run amok', but it continues to ban 'tad'.

Its origins are mysterious. It appears first in the 1877 edition of Bartlett's *Dictionary of the American Language*, defined as a small boy – or an old man. Early in the twentieth century it meant 'a small amount', as in 'give him a tad to eat'. Finally it settled down as 'slightly': in, for instance, 'a tad unhappy'.

Some derive it from 'tadpole', encouraged by a single reference in Shakespeare's nasty *Titus Andronicus* to someone spearing a human 'tadpole' on his rapier's point. But 'tadpole' itself is a zoologically ill-informed extension of 'tadde', an Old English word for toad.

Toads in general get a bad press in English: 'anything hateful or loathsome', according to the *OED*. And yet, in the nineteenth century, 'toad' was an affectionate term for children, just as 'tad' was in the US. Their word, as so often, seems to represent the survival of an English form that had survived in dialect over there.

And is 'tad' unnecessary? A bit, a little, a touch, a jot. What do you think?

Task

A young woman appeared on television to discuss the conflicting demands of work and marriage. 'I'm not multitasking,' she moaned. Perhaps she needed upgrading.

What makes a person see herself as a kind of computer? In computing, a 'task' is a basic unit of programming. When it appears to be able to handle many such jobs simultaneously, the computer is said to be 'multitasking'.

'Multitasking' is generally achieved by making the processor switch its attention from job to job so fast that it seems to be doing everything simultaneously. Parents of young children will know the feeling.

Considering what an unwelcome imposition a 'task' can be, it is perhaps not surprising that, historically, it is the same word as 'tax'. Both came from the Latin verb *taxare*. In Middle English, they meant the same thing: a demand by your feudal superior.

The difference, which emerged slowly in the fourteenth and fifteenth centuries, was that a tax was paid in money, whereas a 'task' required only your hard work. Later that feudal element disappeared, and a 'task' became any kind of onerous duty or work.

There have also been various specialized uses. In Victorian public schools, a 'task' was a set lesson or a piece of homework. Modern teachers, too, fret about keeping children 'on task' in class.

It was also a favoured word in twentieth-century psychology, meaning not only the procedure at the centre of an experiment but also, by extension, mental work generally. It seems likely that this is the source of the adoption of the word by the computer scientists, seeking to describe the machine's thought process.

People's apparent desire to compare themselves with computers is surprising, but nothing new. Their grandparents were happy to describe themselves as 'steaming ahead' or 'really motoring' when those were new and exciting technologies.

Becoming 'multitasking' is difficult enough for a computer, let alone a human being. And computers are a lot easier to fix when they break down.

Themed

From a description of a new restaurant: 'It will be lively, informal and lightly themed'. And that's only the food.

Things are increasingly 'themed'. Restaurants are, of course, but also pubs, clubs, motorway service stations, charity events and even the meals in your staff canteen. The chef takes a package trip to the Caribbean and it's goat curry and plantains for a week.

That 'lightly themed' restaurant will probably attempt to pass itself off as a New Orleans nightclub, or a Tex-Mex diner, or it might have a stab at Provençal or Catalan. But it will always remain British at heart. More's the pity.

To 'theme' is to redesign a place of entertainment according to some Big Idea, either about Abroad or about something Cultural. You might call a restaurant Molly Bloom's, and ensure that the dishes were inspired by Ulysses. You would probably not try this with the works of Will Self.

It's all a development of the 'theme park', an expression first recorded in the US in 1960, when it took over from such rivals as 'kiddieland'. 'Theme restaurants' arrived shortly after that. They came here in the late 1970s, as the nation struggled manfully to overcome the handicap of not being American.

'Theme pub' and 'theme restaurant' surfaced here in 1983, although four years earlier the humorist Simon Brett had imagined 'Great Expectations, a restaurant themed wittily around the works of Dickens'.

'Theme' seems to have come originally from the Greek *thema*, meaning a proposition. It appeared in English in about 1300, meaning the topic of a discussion. In the sixteenth century, however, it became the word for a school composition, and remained thus for 400 years, until the word 'essay' replaced it, in Britain at least.

In the US, however, schoolchildren continue to compose 'themes'. The American 'theme park' is an amusement park developed with the same relentlessness as any school project. Is it any wonder that they are such hard work?

Toerag

Here's the television presenter Mark Lamarr on 'his pal' Chris Evans: 'He thinks he's a genius but I'd say he's a toerag.' Aren't celebrity friendships touching?

Since the late nineteenth century, a 'toerag' has been a layabout, tramp or disreputable person. The *OED*'s first citation in this sense, from 1875, connects it with circus life: 'Toe rags is another expression of contempt . . . used . . . chiefly by the lower grades of circus men, and the acrobats who stroll about the country, performing at fairs.' These days it is used without affection by the police to refer to those they encounter in the line of duty.

But what was a 'toerag' before it was a person? A rag wrapped around the toes? Such an object does feature in an 1862 study of convicts, and in later accounts of tramping, notably Orwell's *Down and Out in Paris and London*, which mentions: 'horrid greasy little clouts known as toe-rags which they bind round their toes'. Such accessories might lower you in the eyes of the respectable world – but try drying your socks by the side of the road.

Another theory places the rags *outside* the footwear. Apparently the lowliest London dockers were known as 'toe-rags', because they wore cloths over their boots as they clambered over the grain in ships' holds.

Others insist that the word is not 'toe-rag' at all, but 'tow-rag'. Apparently, 'tow' cloths were used for wiping up all manner of nastiness in nineteenth-century hospitals.

Then there's the suggestion that 'toerag' is really Tuareg, the name of a nation of Saharan nomads. Or perhaps it was something to do with *tau rika rika*, the Maori for slave, often cited as the source of the nineteenth-century Australian 'toe-ragger', a person looked down upon even by tramps.

In the West Country, meanwhile, the distinctive smell of soaking salt cod led to it being called 'toe-rag'. Not greatly popular here, but adored elsewhere. So perhaps Chris Evans needn't feel too bad.

Totem

Totem

If you are a Scot, it may be your own edition of the television news. If you are Old Labour, it may be comprehensive education. If you an Ulster loyalist, it's the Drumcree march.

All of the above are 'totems'. In this cliché, a 'totem' is a rallying point, something to dance around, whooping. All of which would have mystified the Ojibway Indians who gave us the word.

Actually, they call themselves the Anishinaabeg, which means 'Original People'. Ojibway means 'puckered up' and describes the front seam on their moccasins.

To the Ojibway, a 'totem' is an animal (or the spirit of an animal) which gives an Indian clan its name, and with which it shares allegiance and mutual protection. Clan members use the animal's outline as a badge and as a signature. And they refrain from eating it.

The term emerged in a French account of travels in 'Nouvelle France', dated 1609, where a local's familiar spirit is referred to as his *aoutem*. 'Totem' appeared first in 1760, described as a word in Algonquin, a related language to Ojibway. In fact, the root word was probably more like *ote* or *otem*, meaning 'kinship group' in Ojibway, with the 't' bit just meaning 'his'. And it was pronounced 'do-dem'.

However mangled the word, it proved extremely useful. Anthropologists found similar patterns around the world, notably in Australia. Then metaphors arrived. Here's the *Pall Mall Gazette* in 1890: 'The vulgar embroidered smoking-cap, which used to be the distinctive totem of the bazaar debauchee.' His tribal mark, in other words.

'Totem' today has more to do with fantasies about the 'totem pole', common in Westerns but rare in North American Indian society. This has spawned its own cliché. To be 'high on the totem pole' is to have status. But the carvings on the top were often apprentice work. The best were at the bottom, where people could see them. Those 'low on the totem pole' can take comfort from that.

Toxic

Just about everything is 'toxic' these days. Once, the word was restricted to things that might kill you. But if you believe the adverts for beauty products, the world is full of 'toxic chemicals' or 'toxins' that won't end your life but might prevent your skin looking its youthful best.

And there's more. What's a 'toxic bachelor'? Hard to say, but they featured in the relentless New York sitcom *Sex in the City*. Again, they didn't kill anyone or make them ill, but they did make them miserable, at least until the next one came along.

Fundamentally, 'toxic' means poisonous: it is a particularly useful word for writing on bottles of bleach because it doesn't take up much room. 'Toxic' preceded 'toxin', which really means a poisonous protein generated by bacteria or by certain snakes and plants. The mysterious 'toxins' created by modern life, and only detectable by the white-coated experts on the cosmetics counter, rarely fit this definition.

The first word in this group to reach England, in the fifteenth century, was the adjective 'intoxicate', meaning 'smeared with poison'. 'To intoxicate', meaning first to poison and then to render drunk, came a century later. 'Toxic' itself, meaning poisonous, didn't arrive until after the Civil War.

At first, it had no connection with disease, but in nineteenth-century medicine it began to be used for illness caused by poison, either from internal or external sources. An early example was Toxic Insanity. Toxic Shock Syndrome, identified only in 1978, was another illness which helped push 'toxic' to its present notoriety.

The roots of 'toxic', however, lie elsewhere. We can trace it back through French and Latin to the classical Greek phrase *toxicon pharmacon* meaning 'poison for smearing on arrows'. For once the Romans made a mistake. They borrowed *toxicon* to mean poison, but that was the part that meant 'pertaining to arrows'. Too many 'toxins' in their drinking water, no doubt.

Tribe

'Fashion tribes,' says the *Independent*, 'have sprung up from the catwalk, dance and music scenes like vegetables on an allotment.'

'We pigeonhole each other constantly,' it continues, 'and flock to the bars, clubs, shops and restaurants where we will find birds with our own particular feathers.' Mixed metaphors aside, then, a 'tribe' is a group of people with tastes in common.

Among these are the self-styled 'new tribes', whose tastes run to nesting in trees and burrows. According to one member of such a tribe, quoted on its own website, 'A growing body of people in Britain have turned to the ways of indigenous tribal people in order to live in harmony with nature.' Tribal people with cellphones and Internet access, that is.

But 'tribes' were fashionable among materialistic market researchers and advertising folk long before the days of road protest. They wanted a term for the fragments into which the youth market had split, and 'tribes' fitted the bill.

Since the seventeenth century, 'tribe' has been a vaguely derogatory epithet for groups and fraternities. In American criminal slang at the turn of the century, it meant a gang of delinquents. This usage was happily adopted by the hippies in the late 1960s, and it is from this, rather than from anthropology, that the 'tribal' identity of the protestors probably springs.

'Tribes' comes originally from the Latin *tribus*, meaning one of the three political groups of early Rome. Later it was used for the twelve tribes of Israel, and it came into English in early Bible translations.

Technically, members of a tribe should have a common ancestor. The tribes of Israel, for instance, descended from the twelve sons of Jacob. Then ten went missing, only to be identified later as the American Indians, the Kashmiris, the Japanese and the Mormons, among others.

No one has yet identified Britain's tree-dwellers as a lost tribe of Israel. But it is only a matter of time.

Tsunami

An article on one of the newspaper technology pages recently declared that something or other had been the subject of 'a tsunami of publicity'. A new image, but perhaps a bit of an exaggeration.

A 'tsunami' is what we used to call a 'tidal wave'. It's a Japanese word, more accurately transliterated as *tunami*, that combines the words for 'wave' and 'harbour' to denote a wave that starts with an underwater earthquake and ends by creating havoc as it hits land. We learned the word when Japan opened up in the late nineteenth century but we have only recently started using it, for reasons of geographical correctness.

Originally, a 'tidal wave' ('tide wave' before that) was simply the moon's effect on the water, producing a high tide twice a day. But by the middle of the nineteenth century, it had already been misapplied to freak waves of the destructive and dramatic kind, and was already inspiring figurative uses. As early as 1870, Mark Twain was planning to launch his next book on 'a big tidal wave' of publicity.

'Tsunami' underwent a similar transition from the language of geography to the language of journalism in the 1970s. It was then that *Science* magazine in America declared that the Food and Drug Administration was 'swimming through a tsunami of comments' on its drug strategy.

Recently this recondite word has become almost commonplace: certainly commonplace enough to inspire a hit tune by the Manic Street Preachers. But it is especially prized by those who write about technology, as well as those looking for attractive names for pieces of hardware or software. A quick look at the Internet suggests why this might be the case. A common (though inaccurate) metaphor for the business of using the World Wide Web is 'surfing'. And what do you need to surf swiftly, powerfully and enjoyably? Big waves.

Virus

Have you noticed how 'virus' has started to mutate?

We know a 'virus' as something that invades our cells, starts to multiply and then either gives us a bit of a sniffle or kills us. On the one hand, 'justavirus', last resort of the hard-pressed GP; on the other, Ebola.

This would seem to make it an odd word to use in commerce. But viruses are all the rage. Not the computer variety, but 'idea viruses' and 'viral marketing'. These techniques involve using modern communications, from e-mail to mobile phones, to spread your message like something contagious.

This may be irritating – how much junk mail can the system stand? – but does it deserve such a nasty name? In the original Latin, *virus* meant slime, poison or stench. In English, from *c.* 1600, it meant the venom of a snake. Adopted by medicine, it meant the pus oozing from a sore.

At the end of the nineteenth century, Louis Pasteur used it to mean the contagious agent contained within the aforementioned secretion. He was actually looking at a bacteria, but the usage survived to be applied to 'viruses' when they were subsequently identified.

Recently, a process of analogy has given us the computer 'virus', a small program that multiplies itself, spreads and does damage. The idea appeared first in science fiction and then, in the early 1980s, some bright spark built one as an experiment. More malicious variants soon followed.

Richard Dawkins, the evolutionary biologist and hammer of the clerics, used a similar analogy when he said that religion was a 'virus'. Fair or not, this particular comparison has found a useful evolutionary niche in the vocabulary of abuse.

But to a certain class of scientist, 'virus' is not an insult. They admire them, both in death-dealing and data-trashing form, for their ingenuity and relentless will to survive. In this context, consider also 'media virus', a recent expression for any particularly irritating television presenter.

Watershed

You know you're getting old when something smutty on the television makes you consult your watch to ensure it is 'after the watershed'. But what about when you start wondering what a 'watershed' is?

Obviously, it's not a shed full of water. All those nails and knotholes would seem destined to leak. And yet . . . Here's a reference in a book of 1859, about Brittany: 'In a water-shed at the end are two women washing.' A shed *containing* water, in other words, where nineteenth-century Bretonnes did their laundry. What does that tell us about the exquisite calculations of twenty-first-century television executives?

There is more than one 'watershed'. We use the word as a synonym for 'turning point'. That would make sense if, say, a 'watershed' meant the moment when a river bursts its banks and inundates surrounding areas with dirty water, smut, foul language, exhibitionism and drag artistry. But it doesn't.

But it *is* a geographical term. A 'watershed' is just a patch of high ground separating valleys that drain into two different rivers. It's a line on a map. No bursting banks, no floods, no drag queens.

The word is really the German *Wasserscheide*, translated into English at the end of the eighteenth century. The first figurative uses, at the end of the nineteenth, were geographically correct. Longfellow spoke of midnight as the 'Watershed of Time, from which the streams of Yesterday and Tomorrow take their way'. In other words, a dividing line.

In 1962, though, the BBC announced its 'watershed policy', a 9.30 p.m. divide (then) between programmes suitable for children and those which were not. Given the policy's purpose, the word soon acquired new associations. In journalistic cliché, it became a barrier or dam that people were constantly 'reaching', 'passing' or 'crossing'.

The 'opening of the floodgates' featured heavily, especially in the *Daily Mail*. At which point the metaphorical waters were thoroughly muddied.

Way

It's odd how fashionable expressions find their way to what you might imagine to be the most sheltered sectors of society. Even infant schoolchildren have been known to declare things 'way cool'.

Fifteen years ago, such expressions were trendy among the vacuous Valley Girls of California. Five years ago, they were hip among teenagers and older schoolchildren. Now they're heard in the nursery.

Of course, they get it slightly wrong. As well as 'way cool', these five-year-olds say things are 'way nice' and that they're 'way tired' and 'way hungry'. Technically similar to 'way cool', but not quite idiomatic.

The use of 'way' as an intensifying adverb to replace 'very' is American, but older than you might think. In the early nineteenth century, 'way' was first coupled to prepositions to indicate distance: 'way over there', 'way down South', 'way off course'. Another example was 'way out'. At first this applied to people who lived on the frontier: by the 1950s it meant people who didn't share your affection for magnolia paintwork.

All these 'way' idioms came about through the erosion of the initial 'a' in 'away', common also in northern English and Scots. Indeed, 'away' was synonymous with 'way' for many years. As late as the first decade of the twentieth century you could read that manufacturers were 'away behind with their orders'.

Thereafter 'away' gave way to 'way', as the word settled down to mean little more than 'much' or 'very'. All of which is some distance from the word's roots. It means path or road, and is found in the earliest Anglo-Saxon texts, with similar words in other Germanic languages. Indeed, similar words are found in Latin, Greek and Sanskrit, making 'way' about as old as our words get.

A 'way' need not be a physical path, however. It can be a psychological or philosophical journey, such as New Labour's 'Third Way', opened for traffic in the early 1990s but now rarely mentioned. Perhaps it has closed for repairs.

Whistle-blower

There has never been a better time to be a whistle-blower. Once, these public servants exposed skullduggery and had their lives ruined. Now there's a law to protect them and every chance that Hollywood will want to tell their story, especially if they worked in deep secrecy before discovering the public's right to know.

The expression is American, first spotted in about 1970. A 'whistle-blower' is someone who nobly draws attention to a malpractice in big business or government, usually by going to the media.

In the US, the practice was rapidly institutionalized. It introduced 'whistle-blower' laws, protecting those who speak out. What's more, many organizations have their own 'whistle-blower' helplines, encouraging their own employees to speak out about malpractice – but not very loudly, and preferably without telling the outside world. It works that way here too. The government's Public Interest Disclosure Act of 1998 allows disclosure to the outside world but only after internal channels have been exhausted.

But what kind of whistle is being blown here? Factory? Penny? Or referee's? It seems to be the latter. The phrase 'to blow the whistle' on something or someone is first recorded in 1934, in Wodehouse's *Right Ho, Jeeves*.

This is not quite the same as modern 'whistle-blowing'. Wodehouse talks about the 'whistle being blown' on a public speech, so it is apparent that the metaphor meant to stop something, rather than to raise attention to it. In other words, it is what the referee does when he raises his Acme Thunderer to his lips at the end of ninety minutes.

In the modern version, however, the metaphor clearly relates to the referee 'blowing up' to indicate that he has seen an infraction. This is, perhaps, more realistic. 'Whistle-blowers' may alert people to things that have happened, but they are usually in no position to stop anything.

Mind you, what some recent whistle-blowers seem to be blowing is their own trumpet.

Whoops-a-daisy!

Did you see *Notting Hill*? Did you notice the mistake? I don't mean the script's assertion that it is possible to support a large house and a business in W11 by selling a couple of guidebooks a week. Nor am I questioning the casting of the male lead.

It's more of a verbal error. In one scene, Hugh Grant's character struggles to climb some railings into a private garden. Meanwhile the ineffably beautiful American film star played by Julia Roberts (a risky piece of casting) hops lightly over.

As he falls, Grant says this: 'Whoops-a-daisies!' Then he says it again. 'Whoops-a-daisies!' Plural. Roberts immediately sees how quaint, old-fashioned and yet endearing Grant is and kisses him. You'll probably want to fast-forward that bit.

Has anyone, ever, said 'whoops-a-daisies', except perhaps Richard Curtis, the writer, or Hugh Grant, who may have tweaked the line? The expression is surely 'whoops-a-daisy', or 'whoopsiedaisy'? What's more, while it is old-fashioned, it's not even English. It is recorded first in this form in a *New Yorker* cartoon of 1925 as 'Whoopsie Daisy!'

The original expression, usually associated with the idea of picking up fallen toddlers rather than lovesick booksellers, goes back to the eighteenth century. Then it was 'upaday', 'up a-dazy' or 'up-a-daisey'. No daisies are involved: that's just a way of stretching the word 'up' to accompany an action.

'Up-a-daisy' disappeared for a while, surviving only in dialect, notably in Yorkshire. There the 'up' was pronounced more like 'oop': so when it came back, as 'upsadaisy' or 'upsidaisy', early in our century, it was really 'oopsidaisy'.

This new version, recorded first in Leeds, spread across the English-speaking world, with 'oops-a-daisy' as perhaps the most common spelling. In the States, they had their own ideas. After 'Whoopsie Daisy!', the exclamations 'whoops' and 'oops' soon followed.

These days few people bother with 'whoops' or 'whoops-a-daisy' when they fall: they swear. But these expressions do have their uses when talking to very small children – or very big stars.

Win-win

A survey showed that 65 per cent of office workers use arcane corporate jargon in meetings. It makes them feel in control, and baffles everyone else. It's a 'win-win' scenario, they think.

But a 'win-win' situation is not, as many people think, one in which a single action gives you two competitive advantages. It's a transaction in which both parties benefit.

The phrase has its origins in the field of game theory, which began during the last war when it was used in anti-submarine strategy. In 1944, mathematician John von Neumann and economist Oskar Morgenstern first codified the subject. They divided games into two categories: 'zero-sum games', like Snap, in which for one person to win the other has to lose; and 'non-zero-sum games' in which both parties can 'win' by co-operation.

In life, their real subject, things come in both categories. A simple pay negotiation, whereby any money saved in wages belongs to the employer, is a zero-sum game. A self-financing productivity deal, in which employees are paid more because they generate more income, is a non-zero-sum game, or a 'win-win' game. You can see why 'win-win' is so fashionable in modern Britain.

From the beginning, game theory was influential in management and personnel circles, leading to a string of books proposing 'win-win strategies' in everything from international relations to marriage, possibly a greater challenge.

'Win-win' was already a cliché in American business by the early 1980s. When it arrived here, c. 1990, it was still unfamilar enough to us to need inverted commas, but it has since surfaced in such fields as law, computer science and evolutionary biology. A book called *Nonzero: the Logic of Human Destiny* even proposed it as the meaning of life.

As a piece of business jargon, though, it is under threat. The Americans are testing a bigger, better replacement. The 'win, win, win' situation has already been spotted in their business press.

Window

'I'm having a bit of trouble with Windows,' says Andy in Accounts. 'I'll see to it when I have a window,' says Tim in Technical Support, going back to looking out of the 'window'.

Three types of 'windows': Microsoft's computer operating system, called 'Windows' because it divides the screen into a series of rectangular panels; a bit of time, a gap in someone's diary; and a glass pane covering a hole in a building.

'Window' in the latter sense has been with us for 800 years, although for some of that we had to manage without PVC-U. Originally 'window' was the Old Norse *vindauga*, meaning 'wind-eye'. Poetic, isn't it? Certainly more so than the word it replaced, the Old English *eyethurl*, meaning 'eye-hole'.

Recently other openings, literal and figurative, have been called 'windows'. A key development was the 'window' envelope, with its little cellophane panel, introduced early in the twentieth century and widely ignored ever since.

Technical Support's diary 'window' proves to have impressive origins. Scientists would use the word 'window' to mean the gap in a continuous spectrum of something, for instance, radiation. The idea was adapted by the first space scientists. They spoke of the 'launch window': a period of time suitable for lighting the blue touchpaper.

But by the late 1970s the mood had changed. Now a 'window of opportunity' became a period when your enemy's nuclear missiles, or your own, were vulnerable to attack. And to think we use a 'window' to mean a good time for a gossipy lunch.

And what of those computer 'Windows'? The term originated in the early 1960s, meaning using the whole screen as a 'window' to view something larger. But modern 'windows', developed by Xerox in the 1970s and first marketed in Apple's Macintosh, are lots of little screens.

Interestingly, that wasn't the only term for them. Would Bill Gates be where he is today if he'd had to sell us Microsoft 'Viewports'?

Wizard

Wizard

When Black & Decker christened a new power tool 'Wizard', they weren't so much promising magical results as joining a trend. There are, for instance, all those 'wizards' you find in your computer, not to mention the school-age versions currently mesmerizing young (and not so young) readers.

In the past, a new DIY tool would have been called something sensible, like PD135B, say. In general, they are no more capable of sorcery than software 'wizards', who never quite compensate for the essential unhelpfulness of the programs they inhabit.

The vogue for wizardry can safely be blamed on a chap with round glasses, lank hair and a gloomy expression. No, not that one. These 'wizards' have more to do with Bill Gates than Harry Potter.

The proof is on the Internet, where 'web wizards', 'HTML wizards' and 'Gif wizards', whatever they are, easily outnumber 'marketing wizards', 'business wizards' and 'savings wizards'.

A 'wizard', in its fifteenth-century origins, was a 'wise man', just like a 'dullard' is a 'dull man'. It meant someone wise by profession rather than by reputation: a philosopher or seer. In some translations, the Three Kings were 'wizards'.

Later it became associated with the occult. The King James Bible, for instance, recommends that 'wizards' are stoned to death, something that has yet to find reflection in the Potter stories.

In the nineteenth century, however, the title 'wizard' was adopted by music-hall conjurers, who are still called that in the US. Safely trivialized, it became an affectionate term for anyone with advanced skills, from the 'Welsh Wizard' and the 'Wizard of Dribble' to The Who's 'pinball Wizard'.

Frightening occult 'wizards' live on in folklore, horror and the 'sword and sorcery' games enjoyed by American computer-science students in the 1970s and 1980s. Inevitably, a person with special computer skills was hailed by them as a 'wizard', particularly someone who knew how to manage the horribly complex Unix system. Compared with that, DIY is child's play, Black & Decker or no.

Workaround

Having trouble with your computer? Well, it's probably got a bug, or a glitch, or hardware 'issues'. But don't worry, there is a 'workaround'. Luckily for you.

The idea of the 'workaround' first made it into the public consciousness when the nation's systems managers emerged from obscurity to declare that, although they couldn't guarantee anything, they didn't think the Millennium Bug would actually bring civilization to an end.

The reason for that, they said, was that 'workarounds are in place'. Of course, nobody was reassured. Everybody knew some sane and highly informed computer programmer who had taken wife, children and attack dog to an underground bunker in Orkney. What's more, 'workaround' sounded like a 'kickaround' or a 'runaround', ad hoc and amateurish.

In all these words a prepositional verb has mysteriously become a noun. They have no common origin, but people have found them useful, so they have caught on.

'Workaround' has the jaunty antipodean air of 'walkabout', but it is not Australian. It is, as you might expect, computer hackers' slang. Where better to look for elucidation than the numerous online Internet glossaries?

Here's what the excellent *New Hacker's Dictionary* (www.tuxedo.org/ēsr/jargon/html) has to say: '1. A temporary kluge [or 'kludge', meaning a 'clumsy fudge'] used to bypass, mask, or otherwise avoid a bug or misfeature in some system. 2. A procedure to be employed by the user in order to do what some currently non-working feature should do.'

In other words, precisely what our systems people were saying. There might be a little bit of trouble, but they'd put their 'workarounds' in place and we'd be able to carry on as usual. And the weird thing is, they were right.

So next time you can't print an important document, and Technical Support say they have a workaround, you'll just have to believe them. Won't you?

Wuss

When do we know a word has taken root here? When it appears in Hansard? Or on *The Archers*?

No contest, is it? We know 'wuss' is part of British English because it makes regular appearances in the snarling dialogue of David Archer, Ambridge's not-so-young farmer. And the other day it even appeared in a book review.

We know what 'wuss' means by the company it keeps, just as we did with 'wimp'. Which, as it happens, means much the same thing. But we know little else. The venerable *OED* thinks it's an accented form of 'worse'. As in: 'They told me things could only get better, but they're getting wuss.' Get hip, Granddad.

More recent general dictionaries tell us it is a term that deliberately insults the weak and ineffectual, that it is American, late twentieth century and of unknown origin. We could have worked all that out for ourselves, as well as what the dictionaries tend not to say, that it carries an implication of effeminacy.

Jonathon Green, in his *Cassell Dictionary of Slang*, bravely suggests that 'wuss' comes from combining 'wimp' and 'pussy', both well-known American terms of abuse. 'Pussy' in this sense is at least sixty years old, both here and in the US. 'Wimp', meanwhile, is a tired 1970s insult in need of replacement.

Leaving 'wimp' aside, it is not unknown for an initial 'p' to turn into 'w': consider 'woofter' from 'poofter'. But there must be a better explanation. Tony Thorne, in his *Bloomsbury Dictionary of Contemporary Slang*, notes that 'wuss' is heard in Wales as a cheery term of address. 'Hiya, wuss,' he quotes. 'How's it going?' He derives it from the Welsh *gwas*, meaning 'servant'.

Intriguing, but surely no more than a coincidence. The word must be American and teenage. Think Beavis and Butthead, who once made the amusing observation that 'England is the place where everyone talks like a wuss.'

No longer. These days we talk like Americans.

Xmas

A curious superstition is abroad, suggesting that 'Xmas', the shortened version of Christmas, is in some way unchristian or worse.

I once heard about a row in a square-dancing club, after the
chairman had used the four-letter word in his posters for the annual
festive dance. His reasoning was simply that if you only use four big
letters, rather than nine small ones, people can read the notices.

Barely had they gone up, however, than someone demanded a
felt pen to amend the lettering on account of Xmas's 'anti-Christian'
nature. A strong charge indeed, satanic connections being frowned
upon in the closely regulated world of American square dancing.

But this was not the first time this particular hobby horse had
been round the paddock. Nor is the aggrieved member – let us call
him Mr X – alone. Quite a few people seem to have become
convinced that the 'x' in 'Xmas' 'crosses out' the word's Christian
identity.

They are, however, making a mistake. 'X' is a fascinating and
useful letter, except perhaps if you are playing Scrabble. Standing
alone, it means 'wrong', 'I'd like this one', 'dirty or violent', 'I've
signed this despite being unable to write', 'multiply by', 'dig here for
treasure', 'kiss' and more, including 'name withheld for legal reasons'.

But it also stands for Christ, and Christian, and it has done since
Anglo-Saxon times. Those converting the heathen English to
Christianity wrote the word 'Crist', from the Latin *Christus*. But
their abbreviations, used for things like 'Christian' and 'christening',
were based on the Greek original, spelt *Xristos*, with the initial 'x'
pronounced as a breathy 'kh'.

There is a *Xres maesse* recorded in the Anglo-Saxon chronicle
of 1100, but our simple 'Xmas' didn't become fixed until the
mid-eighteenth century. It's been with us ever since, without once
attracting suspicion. In other words, Xmas is at least as Christian as
Christmas, although perhaps that isn't saying much.

OTHER PAN BOOKS
AVAILABLE FROM PAN MACMILLAN

JOHN MORRISH
FRANTIC SEMANTICS   0 330 37667 5   £5.99

MICHAEL MEPHAM

THE DAILY TELEGRAPH GIANT GENERAL
KNOWLEDGE CROSSWORD BOOK   0 330 48683 7   £4.99

THE DAILY TELEGRAPH SECOND GIANT GENERAL
KNOWLEDGE CROSSWORD BOOK   0 330 48982 8   £4.99

All Pan Macmillan titles can be ordered from our website,
www.panmacmillan.com, or from your local bookshop
and are also available by post from:

Bookpost, PO Box 29, Douglas, Isle of Man IM99 1BQ
Credit cards accepted. For details:
Telephone: 01624 836000
Fax: 01624 837033
E-mail: bookpost@enterprise.net
www.bookpost.co.uk

Free postage and packing in the United Kingdom

Prices shown above were correct at the time of going to press.
Pan Macmillan reserve the right to show new retail prices on covers
which may differ from those previously advertised in the text
or elsewhere.